DREAM SECRETS

Unlocking the Mystery of Your Dreams

Lucy Gillis

Consultant
John Suler, Ph.D.

Publications International, Ltd.

Lucy Gillis is coeditor of *The Lucid Dream Exchange,* an online newsletter, and writes a monthly column for *Electric Dreams,* an online magazine. Her dream-related writing and poetry have appeared in numerous magazines and newsletters including *Reality Change* and *Perspectives.*

John Suler, Ph.D., is a psychology professor at Rider University. His past publications have focused on psychotherapy, mental imagery, and the relationship between Eastern philosophy and Western psychology. He is currently a consulting editor for three online psychology journals.

Louis Weber, CEO
Publications International, Ltd.
7373 North Cicero Avenue
Lincolnwood, Illinois 60712

Manufactured in U.S.A.

8 7 6 5 4 3 2 1

ISBN: 0-7853-5500-6

Contents

INTRODUCTION
Dream On

Learn more about yourself and your behavior through dream interpretation. For those who choose to explore their dreams, the truth is out there. What do your dreams reveal?

There is no such thing as "just a dream." Even if you wake up thinking a dream means nothing, or if you cannot remember your dream at all, your dream self never fails to send messages in a constant effort to support and guide you. These messages are beneficial; they are your brain's ways of helping you improve various areas of your life. With practice, you can learn how to explore your dreams fully and apply them to your life, using them for ideas, advice, encouragement, and inspiration.

In fact, dreams have been credited throughout history as the sources of discoveries, inventions, inspirations, warnings, and cures. In recent times, medical and scientific breakthroughs such as the discovery of insulin were the results of information given in dreams. Even Albert Einstein claimed a dream inspired his theory of relativity.

You are your own best dream reader. Because your dream self is speaking to you, it strives to get the messages across in symbols and scenes that you can relate to personally. And that is the secret—the key that unlocks your world of dreams. Your dream symbols are not meaningless or sent to confuse you. They are made up of elements of your life experiences. Your dream self wants you to understand your dreams and tries to communicate with you in ways you will understand. When you learn the language of your own dreams and figure out how your mind uses associations, symbols, and figures of speech, you can discover the meanings of your dreams.

Show your dream self that you are interested in learning your personal dream language. Respect your dreams and place value on them. Your dream self is like an acquaintance you occasionally converse with. If you show an interest in the conversations, they will become more engaging and your acquaintance will offer more detail and information. Make your dream self more than an acquaintance; make it your friend.

Your dreaming mind can help you tap into talents and abilities you may not be aware you possess. With dream interpretation, you can learn more about yourself and your behavior. You can reduce stress in your life, gain insight into personal problems, find ways to solve problems, and enhance your creative abilities. In working with your dreams, you will gain more confidence as you learn more about yourself.

So dream on!

In the Rhythm of the Night

*Everyone dreams, every night, whether we
remember dreaming or not. We spend a third of
our lives asleep in silent nocturnal cycles.*

A NIGHT'S SLEEP

Each night, when sleeping, your body does more than
just lie there—it enters a cycle of sleep. Approximately
every 90 minutes, it shifts from light sleep to deep sleep
back to light sleep, repeating patterns four to six times
depending on the total amount of time asleep.

Your body bounces between NREM (nonrapid eye
movement) and REM (rapid eye movement) sleep. It
starts in NREM sleep and visits the four stages that make
up NREM sleep before heading to REM sleep. The four
NREM stages and REM are explained below.

✿ Stage One: As your body drifts off to sleep, it enters
Stage One sleep. Your muscles relax, your body temperature and blood pressure decrease slightly, and your
breathing begins to slow down. This stage is a light
stage of sleep, and it is easy to be awakened from it.

A phenomenon called *hypnagogia* may make it
even harder for you to fall deep into sleep in this
stage. Hypnagogia is characterized by hallucinations
that cause vivid images and sounds, body jerks, and

sensations of falling. It's almost as if your body were fighting sleep.

✿ Stage Two: When you sleep through Stage One, you'll head on to Stage Two and drift deeper into sleep. Most sleepwalking and talking occur at this stage. Again, it seems like your body isn't quite ready to sleep—to be still and silent—but it's losing the fight.

✿ Stage Three: At Stage Three, your body takes the fall—into sleep. It's hard for you to be awakened. Your body temperature drops further; your heart rate and breathing slow down even more. Electrical activity surges in the brain during this time.

✿ Stage Four: Your body's down for the count by Stage Four. An electroencephalogram (or EEG machine) would register large, slow brain waves during this period. All body functions slow down. It is very diffi-cult to be awakened at this time, since your body's sensitivity to its surroundings is diminished.

✿ REM: Even though your body may have been in the ring and lost against those four stages, it goes back for more, returning to Stage Three, then Stage Two. But instead of going on to Stage One again and then wak-ing, your body enters REM sleep about 90 minutes after falling asleep. Research has shown that this is when most dreams occur. Your eyes move back and forth very quickly under closed eyelids (remember: REM means rapid eye movement). Electrical activity in your brain acts very similar to your waking brain—it's as if the body were awake and concentrating on something. Some researchers believe that the body is concentrating upon dreams.

In this phase, your heart rate and breathing increase, your brain temperature rises, and oxygen to your brain multiplies. Signs of sexual arousal are evident even if the dream doesn't have sexual content.

Your body also undergoes sleep paralysis, in which muscles are essentially paralyzed—except the eye muscles. Some scientists believe sleep paralysis happens so we will not act out our dreams and possibly hurt ourselves. However, in some sleep disorders, this motor inhibition doesn't work properly. For example, this happens when a person sleepwalks or when a dog "chases rabbits" while it sleeps.

ALL SLEEP CYCLES ARE NOT THE SAME

During the first part of the night, much of the time will be spent in Stage Four sleep. It is believed that most of your body's rest and rejuvenation takes place in Stage Four sleep. When we don't get enough Stage Four sleep, we wake up tired. The time spent in Stages Three and Four decreases as you continue sleeping, allowing you to spend more time in REM, or dreaming, sleep.

Morning dreams are more vivid and longer than dreams from earlier in the night because each time you cycle through to REM sleep, it lasts a little longer than it did before. By the morning of a good night's sleep, REM sleep lasts from 25 to 45 minutes.

STRANGE (EYE-OPENING) HAPPENINGS

When you are waking up, a phenomenon known as *hypnopompia* may be experienced. This is similar to hypnagogia from Stage One sleep. You may experience hallucinations, such as feeling great pressure on your chest or feeling like you are underwater. Sometimes it feels and sounds as if someone has entered the room and sat on the bed beside you. You may also wake with a jerk and feel like you have fallen. Essentially, in hypnopompia, the mind is awake before the body is. If you experience hypnopompia when trying to wake up, don't struggle;

A Long-Distance House Call

Archaeologist and radio broadcaster Tudor Pole became very ill and suffered a high fever while working in Egypt. One evening, while he dreamed, he believed he heard someone knocking on his door. He thought he was then awake. He saw a doctor by his bed, dressed in a black cloak and top hat. The doctor gave Pole a potion to drink and then left. Pole drank the liquid. When he woke the next day, he was fully recovered from his illness. Later, when he returned to Britain, Pole broadcasted an appeal over the radio for this doctor to get in touch with him. Soon afterward, a Scottish doctor contacted him and told him that he often traveled during his sleep to those who needed him.

just remain calm and relaxed, and very soon your body will awaken and you will be able to move.

Many people don't recall episodes of hypnagogia and hypnopompia, and sleep and wake without incidence. But for people who do remember, these experiences can be very scary—especially for those who don't understand that they are natural parts of the sleep cycle.

DARE TO DREAM

If you were to become sleep-deprived, and therefore REM-deprived, you would not dream. You would experience a loss of memory, fatigue, irritability, and difficulty in concentrating. For instance, many new moms and dads experience this! A crying baby can really disrupt a night's sleep. If the parents were to get a night of only NREM sleep—if baby's cries awake them each time REM begins (babies don't quite grasp the concept of timing; they just physically grasp everything else)—the parents would become forgetful, tired, irritable, and unable to concentrate. The next time they slept after being REM-deprived (maybe around the time baby went off to college), their bodies would spend more time in REM sleep to make up for lost time.

Research has shown extreme dream deprivation can cause people to enter the REM stage while awake, inducing hallucinations and, in effect, dreaming while awake.

A Night in a Sleep Laboratory

Sleep laboratories perform polysomnography, the science of sleep study. If you were to have your sleep monitored for one night, you would sleep with electrodes placed on various parts of your body. These sensors would monitor brain waves, heartbeat, eye movements, muscle activity, as well as respiration and blood oxygen levels. A polysomnograph would produce a graph-like representation of the electrical signals of your body. If you slept for a total of eight hours, the polysomnograph would produce tracings that would stretch for approximately a quarter of a mile.

A LITTLE R&R

It is not entirely clear why people dream, but many theories presume it is to assist the body with its resting, repairing, and rejuvenation. Some people believe we dream for psychological reasons also: to reexamine the day's events, to reduce and relieve stress, and to provide an outlet for emotional release.

Whatever the reason behind dreaming, it seems obvious that it is an essential part of maintaining physical and mental health. Let's take a closer look at what our dreams do for us.

CHAPTER TWO

Dream Aids

Whether you remember fragments of your dreams or don't remember your dreams at all, you can improve or activate your dream recall.

A PICTURE IS WORTH A THOUSAND WORDS

The subconscious is like a huge database filled with intimate details, a warehouse of personal history. But it is even more than that; it is an active part of personality, working to give knowledge, advice, solutions, and encouragement through feelings, inspiration, hunches, and dreams.

The part of the subconscious that works through dreams (the dream self) sends messages as symbols and images. These images explain ideas or situations in a visual language.

So why don't we dream in words? For one thing, participating in an event provides a more meaningful understanding than just reading about it. Plus, visual images remain in the memory longer. They are also better at capturing and stirring emotions. Which do you remember more: the sitcom you watched last night on TV or the last article on page two of yesterday's newspaper? As the saying goes, a picture is worth a thousand words.

When you try to remember your dreams, your dream self responds by providing more detailed and meaningful dreams.

USE YOUR IMAGINATION

You can stimulate your dream recall with the following simple exercise. Choose an event that occurred during your day, and pretend it was a dream. Write it down in the present tense, reliving it as you write. For example, suppose you write about your morning commute to work. Include as much detail as you can remember. You may begin by asking yourself some questions:

✧ What time is it when I leave?
✧ What am I wearing?
✧ Is it a sunny or a cloudy day?
✧ What day of the week is it?
✧ What kind of mood am I in?
✧ Do I speak with anyone?
✧ Do I travel alone?
✧ What time do I arrive?

Thinking about, remembering, and recording these details as though they took place in a dream helps train your mind to remember your dreams, and writing out an event mimics writing in a dream journal, an important tool in dream work.

Another exercise is to suggest to yourself that you will remember your dreams. Select a phrase you are com-

Following Tracks

Harriet Tubman, who helped free hundreds of slaves through the Underground Railroad, was often guided by her dreams. She avoided danger and found safe routes for the fugitives with the help of her dreams.

fortable with, perhaps something like "I remember my dreams easily." Keep it short and positive. You will achieve better results when the statement is in the present tense instead of implying success in the future.

You may want to choose a trigger to remind you to repeat your phrase. For instance, every time you look at your watch or at a clock, repeat your phrase (either aloud or in your mind), as though it is already an established fact. While doing so, picture yourself writing out your dreams.

You may also put little sticky notes as reminders wherever they will be noticed often, such as on your bathroom mirror, on your computer, or on your fridge. You can write your phrase on the notes or leave them blank; it doesn't matter, as long as they serve to remind you of your exercise.

SLEEP EASY

Another way to let your dream self know that you are receptive to your dreams is by preparing your sleeping environment and yourself. Avoid large amounts of alcohol or food before sleep, as they affect the sleep cycle and dreaming. If you are the type of person who can't concentrate well in a messy room, tidy up before sleeping. Fluff your pillows, straighten your covers, and wear loosely fitting sleepwear. This way, your sleep will not be distracted by small annoyances. Also, make sure the room temperature is comfortable.

Once your bodily needs are met, set your alarm to wake you about 15 minutes earlier than usual so you will have time to write out your dream notes. If possible, wake to gentle music instead of an alarm. Sometimes, being startled awake may wipe out dream memories.

If you rely on a loud alarm to wake you, don't despair! You can train your mind to remember your dream, regardless of the jarring noise, simply by suggesting to yourself that, when you hear the alarm, the dream will remain fresh in your mind. If you'd like, you may incorporate this suggestion into your reminder phrase.

Journaling

You should also prepare a dream journal. A journal is necessary, not only because it helps you track recurring elements, but because the act of recording your dreams makes them important to the dream self.

Prepare your journal however you like. Some people prefer fancy journals. Others choose a notebook or looseleaf pages to be inserted into a binder. It's a good idea to leave a few blank pages at the beginning of the journal so you can make a table of contents. This will make it easy for you to scan the titles when you're looking for one dream in particular.

Put your dream journal and a pen or a tape recorder close to your bed. Also keep a penlight or small flashlight handy in case you wake in the middle of the night and want to record a dream. The penlight will make it easier for you to fall back to sleep when you're done than turning on the overhead light.

Before you sleep, open your dream journal to a fresh page. At the top of the page, note the city you are in (particularly if you travel a lot), the date, and the time you went to bed. Leave space at the top to title your dream in the morning. Summarize the day's events, as they may influence dream content. Write "I will remember my dreams easily" or whatever phrase you have chosen. If you want, include other notes, such as the mood you are in as you get ready for bed or the state of your health. For an idea of what to include in your dream journal, refer to pages 24–25.

As you drift off to sleep, gently repeat your suggestion to yourself over and over.

Recording Your Dream

When you wake up, lie still, keeping your eyes closed. Often just the act of movement can cause a dream memory to fade and vanish. Think about what is happening in your mind, without attempting to control or manipulate the content. Don't be discouraged if you can't remember immediately. Something may trigger the memory later.

Go over the dream again in your mind. When you are satisfied that you can recall the dream, write it down (or record it on a tape recorder) immediately. Write (or speak) in the present tense, reliving the dream as you record it. Don't worry if you can't remember the order in which events occurred—it doesn't matter if you start at the middle or work your way backward—the important thing is to get the dream recorded.

If you are recording your dream on tape, be sure that you write it down in your dream journal later, because it's easier to review your dreams on paper than on tape. Record as much detail as you can: people, places, colors,

Sensational Dreamwork

Charlotte Brontë, best known as the author of *Jane Eyre,* is said to have used her dreams to help with her writing when she needed to describe something for which she had no personal experience. She would go to sleep wondering what it would be like to experience whatever sensation she needed to depict in her work. When she awoke in the morning, she could clearly remember and describe the sensation as though it had really happened, and she was able to use it in her writing, exactly as it occurred in her dream.

actions, animals, symbols, and emotions. If you don't
have time to write the entire dream, make brief notes.
You can go back later and write down the details.

If you remember only parts when you wake, record
them. They are important, and more information may
come as you write. If you don't remember dreaming anything, note how you felt when you woke. Sometimes this
can help you remember the dream. Be sure that you
write something—anything!—to reinforce the idea of
recording dreams and to remind your dream self that
you truly are interested in receiving dream messages.

When finished, write the time that you woke and
choose an appropriate title for the dream. Don't forget to
congratulate yourself on a job well done! Save a page
after the dream report for interpretation and notes.
Events throughout the day may trigger more memory of
the dream. If this happens, make a note of what you've
just recalled and add it to your journal later.

As you go through your day, repeat your suggestion
as before, and if you didn't recall a dream, write out an
event that happened as though it were a dream. You
might write about how you woke up and tried to recall
your dreams: how you felt in the morning, what you
were wearing, whether you sat up or moved to a desk,
and whether you thought of a title (like "Close, But No
Cigar"). The next time, you may remember more and
write in your journal something like "I awake with a

vague feeling of having been in a sunny place. There is brightness and warmth." You may want to title it something like "No Cigar, But Getting Warmer!"

When it's time to sleep again, repeat the procedure of preparing your sleeping environment and dream journal.

BEFORE COUNTING SHEEP

Before you fall asleep, read over the previous night's dream, remembering it as vividly as you can. This puts you back in touch with your dreaming mind. Recall how you felt when you woke. Also, briefly review your day. Did anything happen that appeared in your dream? Did any of your dream symbols turn up during your day? If so, make brief notes before drifting off to sleep.

It is important to be consistent with your dream journal and keep up with it as much as you possibly can. However, if your lifestyle is not one that can accommodate daily dream writing, choose those days that are better for writing and keep to that routine, even if it is only one or two days a week.

Don't get discouraged if you don't get immediate results! As with learning any skill, dream recall takes time, effort, and patience.

Discover Your Dream Language

Become your own dream oracle by learning your personal dream language.

CRACK THE CODE

Since most everyone dreams in pictures, it is important to learn to understand what these pictures represent. Objects or symbols in dreams can have many meanings depending on how they appear, the environment in which they appear, and, most important, the beliefs and associations the dreamer holds with regard to the symbols.

It is understandable that a lot of symbols will hold the same general meanings for many of us, since millions of people speak the same language, live in the same culture, and are exposed to the same media. For instance, most would agree that a telephone can be regarded as a general symbol of communication.

However, each of us has our own perspective on life, along with our own personal beliefs, experiences, and memories. For instance, water may symbolize refreshment and cleansing to most people, but to the person who nearly drowned at an earlier time in life, water may represent feelings of fear, helplessness, and disaster.

Archetypes

Symbols that are common to many cultures are called archetypes. A few examples are:

- ✿ the mother, who represents birth, nurture, and emotions;
- ✿ the father, who represents a provider and a thinker;
- ✿ the hero, who represents a rescuer and salvation; and
- ✿ the monster, who represents fears.

Figures of Speech

The dream self is very clever and will use pictures to show figures of speech, like puns, slang terms, symbols, and word soundalikes, in much the same way that advertisements do to get our attention. For example, you may be frustrated that Ed won't give you a straight answer. You may dream of throwing a magazine on the floor and seeing Ed dance around it. A woman asks if you've seen Frank. In other words, Ed is "dancing around the issue," and your dream may be telling you to be more frank with Ed and let him know that you need straight answers.

BREAK IT DOWN

In order to decipher a dream, you will need to break it down into smaller elements, but before you do, think it through as a whole. Could there be a literal meaning? Don't dismiss the obvious. Sometimes our dreams are very straightforward and reflect day-to-day concerns.

If there doesn't appear to be an obvious meaning, break the dream into separate elements (*see also* "Elements" on page 25).

✿ How did you feel when you woke up? Usually the mood you were in at the end of a dream will be the mood you feel when you wake up. Did you feel one or several emotions during your dream?

✿ Note the time and location. Did your dream seem to take place in the past, present, or future? Was it daytime? Night? Was the season obvious? How was the weather? Where did the dream take place? Locally or out of town?

✿ Make a list of characters. Note nicknames, too; these can give important clues. Ask yourself if the character reminds you of anyone else. It doesn't matter if the characters are personally known by you, are strangers, or are celebrities. Sometimes we can be quite involved with the lives of celebrities. Maybe you admire how they handle situations, or perhaps you are going through similar circumstances. Also look for animals and animated or cartoon characters. Then take note of yourself. Are you observing the dream, or do you take part in it? Are you yourself, or do you display a radically different personality? What about your age or state of health?

✿ Make a list of the symbols in your dream and where they appear or how they are placed or positioned.

Look for prepositions or "placement" words such as *on, under, behind,* and *beside.* Are any of the symbols moved from place to place during the course of the dream? You might also note if anything is missing that should be there.

☆ Look for activities. What actions were performed, or what motions or travel occurred? One clue to finding activities in your dream report is to look for verbs such as *run, jump, sing, dance,* and *speak.*

☆ Are any figures of speech evident? Look for metaphors, puns, slang terms, and word soundalikes such as *red* for *read, blue* for *blew, dye* for *die,* and *passed* for *past.* Write down any words you feel may be important.

☆ Determine if there is an overall theme to your dream. Was it work-related? What about family issues? Maybe a hobby or interest was the focus. Crafts? Archaeology? Sports? Perhaps the dream points out a dilemma or problem that is on your mind. Your dream may have several themes or it may have no obvious theme at all, so don't be concerned if you can't fit it into a specific category.

☆ Write out any other comments you may have. Does the title you gave the dream give you any clues? Look over the symbols once more. Do any figures of speech stand out now that the dream has been broken down?

DECIPHER THE MESSAGE

Once you've broken the dream down into separate elements, you are ready to begin deciphering the message. What do the symbols mean to you? If you aren't sure, ask yourself what comes to mind when you think of each one. Some meanings will be obvious to you. For symbols you are unsure of, check pages 38–128 to learn some common general meanings.

Don't pressure yourself to come up with an instant interpretation. Be patient. As you become more familiar with your symbols, it will become easier to decode your dream language. You may not understand your dream until later, when something triggers a meaning for you. Some dream messages may make themselves known to you on a subconscious level, appearing as hunches, intuition, or inspiration felt later in the day or even days later.

But how will you know when you have interpreted your dream message correctly? With practice, there will be an instant inner knowing and a feeling of recognition and understanding—you will just know.

Below are a sample dream and interpretation. The dream is from Cathy, who wakes up feeling rushed and frustrated.

Sample Dream

Place: *Townsville*   **Date:** *July 5, 2001*   **Bedtime:** *10:30* P.M.
Day Notes: *Hectic day at work. A meeting that took longer than*

expected delayed my other projects, and I was forced to bring work home; I didn't trust it to junior partners.

Reminder Phrase: *I remember my dreams easily.*

Dream Title: *Trying to Meet Mom for Lunch*

Dream Content: *I have a lunch date with Mom, but I'm late. It's a sunny day as I walk downtown to our favorite restaurant. In the distance, I see Mom standing under an archway. I quicken my pace, but I don't seem to get any closer to her. I am slowed by the heavy package I am carrying. The next time I look ahead, I see Mom standing under a different type of arch. I keep walking toward her, but I get distracted by other things, like looking into the package. A man steps in front of me and tries to give me a clock. I don't want it. He keeps yelling "Take it! Take it!" I walk away, grumbling to myself. Suddenly, I remember my lunch date and am angry for forgetting it. I rush to the restaurant, but I wake before I get there. I feel frustrated when I wake.*

ELEMENTS

Dream Title: *Trying to Meet Mom for Lunch*

Emotions: *Frustration, anxiety, and anger*

Time in Dream: *Daytime*

Season: *Summer*   **Weather:** *Sunny*   **Location:** *Townsville*

Characters: *Mom; me as my present self; man*

Objects/Positions of Objects: *Arch (over Mom); package (in my hands); clock (in man's hands)*

Activities/Events: *Walk; stand; rush; carry; get distracted; look; step out; give; yell; take; grumble; remember; forget; meet for lunch at a restaurant*

Figures of Speech: *"Rest or rant"=restaurant; another type of arch=archetype; clock/"take it"=biological clock, "take some time"*

Overall Theme: *Family meeting*

Other Comments: *In the dream, I am easily distracted, and I feel frustrated when I realize I've forgotten my intent to meet Mom.*

Interpretation

Cathy's dream self is being playful, using "type of arch" to indicate "archetype." Her mother standing under the arch indicates the archetypal mother, or the part of the personality that nurtures. Since she is just standing under these arches, it implies that Cathy's self-nurturing aspect is at a standstill. Her mother in the distance could also point to a feeling of disconnection from her mother or from her own maternal instincts.

All the other action words imply busy-ness, movement, and no rest. Other things distract her and take her mind off meeting with her mother and, therefore, take her mind off nurturing herself. The man, someone that she doesn't know personally, could represent an authority figure trying to give her advice. He repeats himself, indicating that his message is important. The clock represents time, possibly the "biological clock" that keeps ticking. The man's advice to "take it" means that she should "take some time."

Lunch and *restaurant* are two more symbols. They represent sustenance, or nurturing, which she is unable to reach due to distractions and the heaviness of the package she is carrying. The package could symbolize her workload or Cathy's own or imagined child, maybe pregnancy. Her attempt to look into the package could signify her wish to pay more attention to her own children or her wish to have a child.

Cathy's clever dream self may also be asking her if she wants to "rest or rant." It's a play on words represented by the symbol of a restaurant. In other words, does she want to take time for herself, or does she want to keep up a pace that leaves her rushed, grumbling, and frustrated?

The title "Trying to Meet Mom for Lunch" shows that Cathy wants to get in touch with her self-nurturing side.

Dream Catchers

A dream catcher is a Native-American craft. It often looks like a spider's web. It is usually made of wood and leather and is decorated with beads and feathers. It is placed over a dreamer's bed or near a bedroom window. According to legend, bad dreams are caught in the dream catcher, and only good dreams are allowed to slip through to reach the dreamer. In the morning, the first light of day destroys the captured bad dreams.

DREAM-WEAVING

Once you have recorded several dreams and have become more familiar with your dream language, you can begin to review your dreams to see if any symbols or themes recur. You may even have already noticed some recurring patterns. If you have been making a table of contents of your dream titles, scan the list to see if any elements repeat.

Some recurrent dreams are not as easy to spot because the underlying meaning, or theme, is what is recurring—not the symbols or events themselves. If you don't get the message, your subconscious continues to send dreams with the same theme but with different symbols in hopes that you will understand one of them.

Many recurring dreams are quite obvious. These may be like television reruns. They replay the same dream over and over with very little, if any, variance. Your subconscious is trying to tell you something that is important and will keep repeating it until you understand. It may be a past event that replays, which could imply something left unfinished or unresolved. Or you may be obsessing about something that you should deal with and let go. The recurring elements could also be revealing changes in a life issue, acting as a sort of barometer to track progress and setbacks.

Some recurring dreams are like stress indicators. If the same bothersome issues keep coming up throughout your life, the corresponding dream may occur during these times, reminding you that you've been in this situation before.

Not-So-Dreamy Sleep

Unfortunately, many people suffer from recurring dreams that are more than little reminders from their subconscious. Instead, they are anxiety-laden nightmares.

Thanks to the Little People

Writer Robert Louis Stevenson used to have nightmares when he was a child. With practice, he learned to control his dreams and change his nightmares. He stated that he used his dreams to revise his plays and stories in his sleep and that he was assisted by "little people" when he was looking for a new story idea. Indeed, the theme for *The Strange Case of Dr. Jekyll and Mr. Hyde* stemmed from a dream scene that split in two.

According to research, most nightmares are caused by a traumatic event, usually from childhood. The dream replays the event either as it happened or in a symbolic form. (Please note: Experiencing intense or recurring nightmares may indicate a need to seek counseling.)

Nightmares may also represent fears we hold. They are often exaggerated to help get our attention. Sometimes just recognizing the particular fear behind a nightmare can reduce the frequency and intensity of the nightmare.

REALITY CHECK

Make a list, perhaps in the back of your dream journal, of recurring symbols, characters, events, and so on that show up in your dreams. Are the recurring elements appearing in dreams with similar themes?

If you usually have more than one dream per night, cross-check all of your first dreams for similar patterns, then check all of the second dreams together, and so on. Patterns may be obvious, or you may have to seek them out.

After you have been recording your dreams for a while, check dreams that you have on the same night of the week. Weekend dreams may be different than weekday dreams. Or, perhaps, on Wednesdays you go to the gym. Your recently exercised body may relax more deeply when you sleep and may even be conducive to particular dreams. Your dream self may take the opportunity to supply certain messages to you when conditions for good sleep and good recall are available.

Also remember that each dream is not necessarily one story, from start to finish. Some dream messages may be relayed by more than one dream, like a continuing TV story. Often these messages will occur on succeeding nights, or if you recall more than one dream a night, the story may continue over several dreams one night.

Masters of the Secret Things

Certain ancient Egyptian priests were highly esteemed dream interpreters called *Masters of the Secret Things*. Under the guidance of these priests, an individual seeking answers to personal questions would perform elaborate preparations and rituals before sleeping within a dream temple. These rituals were meant to invoke the wisdom of the gods so that the sought-after answers would appear in the individual's dream. The priests would interpret the dreams the following morning.

CHAPTER FOUR
Your Dream Vacation

Have you ever wanted to embark on a wild
adventure but felt it could only
happen "in your dreams"?

EXPAND YOUR HORIZONS

The kind of dream you can incubate (program) is limited
only by your imagination. Many people use dream incubation to find solutions for anything from math problems
to relationship questions. Your incubation procedure can
be elaborate, rich with detail and ritual, or as simple as
repeating a suggestion. The suggestion phrase can be a
question rather than a statement if that is more appropriate, like "How can I improve my golf swing?"

Open the doors to your creative nature by suggesting
dreams that will bring inspiration. Writers, artists, and
other creative individuals have often looked to their
dreams for ideas and insight. Many authors have
dreamed entire stories; others have dreamed particular
scenes, plots, and themes. Some have even dreamed
through the eyes of their characters and have applied the
information they received to their work.

Sometimes athletes practice sports in their dreams,
trying out new techniques. Some people rehearse speeches
to help them overcome their anxiety about speaking in

Paranormal Dreams

Clairvoyant Dream: A dream in which a scene or object is viewed that the dreamer hasn't seen before.

Telepathic Dream: A dream in which communication takes place between the dreamer and another person.

Precognitive Dream: A dream of an event happening or of the dreamer being told what will happen before it actually occurs in waking life.

Prodromal Dream: A dream that foretells physical illness.

public. The dream state can be a safe place to face fears. For instance, if you have a fear of heights, you could incubate a dream in which you climb ladders in an attempt to overcome a fear of heights or a dream in which you have no fear of heights to see how that would feel. Breaking free from fears in your dreams could reduce anxiety in your waking life, even if only temporarily.

If you have a mystical nature and would like to develop your psychic abilities, the dream state is a good place for experimentation. For instance, if you want to develop clairvoyant skills, you could try the following exercise. Have a friend or relative select several pictures from magazines and seal each in a separate envelope. Choose one envelope, then attempt to incubate a dream with the request to your dream self that you will dream about the picture sealed inside. Place the envelope on your nightstand or under your pillow—wherever you like. In the morning, record the dream, open the envelope, and compare the picture with your dream. Make a list of your hits (and misses) in your dream journal.

To test your telepathic abilities, have your friend or family member choose a picture and mentally send you images of the picture on a prearranged evening, just before bedtime. Check with your friend or relative after you have recorded your dream the next day to see how closely your dream corresponds to the picture.

Or perhaps you would like to try something new, something you've never done before. Set your adventurous spirit free by trying bungee jumping or white-water rafting or by singing in a famous band for millions of adoring fans. Your choices are endless!

PLOTTING YOUR COURSE

When you want to get away from it all and enjoy a "dream vacation," it's important to choose a night when you are not too tired and you have no urgent commitments the following morning. For example, it is not a good idea to try to incubate a dream if you have an important meeting the next day, because, most likely, your dream would end up having a work-related theme.

Choose a place you would like to visit. It could be real or imaginary. You could use your dreams like a time machine, or you could travel to another planet or a mythological place—wherever your heart desires!

If you are having difficulty deciding, you may want to go to a travel agency and pick up some brochures. Once you have chosen a locale, find symbols that represent your destination. For instance, suppose you choose Egypt. You may browse through related books or cut out pictures of pyramids or hieroglyphics from magazines or brochures; put them where you will see them often.

Whenever you see the Egyptian pictures, visualize yourself in Egypt. Engage as many of your senses as you can. Imagine touching the stone walls, eating the food, smelling the flowers, hearing the people in the busy markets. Pretend you feel the hot sun on your face and the sand under your feet. Choose a phrase to accompany your visualizations, something like "Tonight I travel to Egypt."

Also, keep a symbol—perhaps another picture, a piece of Egyptian-style jewelry, or an Egyptian figurine—on your nightstand to remind you of your dream intent. Listen to Egyptian music, music that makes you think of

Lest We Forget

Poet Samuel Taylor Coleridge claimed to have had a long and vivid dream that, when he awoke, he began to write out as a poem. However, a visitor interrupted and detained Coleridge for over an hour. When Coleridge returned to his work, he found to his dismay that he could no longer recall the end of the dream, and so the last lines of the famous "Kubla Kahn: Or, A Vision in a Dream" were lost.

Egypt, or music that relaxes you during the day and especially while you get ready to sleep.

If you enjoy ritual, you may want to make your procedure more elaborate, like the people of ancient times did. Find a picture of Serapis, the Egyptian god of dreams, to inspire you. Indulge in a bubble bath surrounded by candles, and listen to relaxing music.

If you aren't fond of ritual or simply haven't the time, remember that the subconscious is very open to suggestion, so simply repeating your phrase and focusing your intent can often be enough to program a dream. Without a doubt, the method most appealing to you will work best.

When getting ready for sleep, prepare your sleeping environment and journal (see pages 14–16); include your suggestion phrase ("Tonight I travel to Egypt") in your dream journal.

In the morning, record your dreams as usual. Since you are programming your dreams, there may not be much, if any, interpretation to do. But be alert, for your dream self may take the opportunity to slip in a message.

Don't be discouraged if you do not get immediate results. Keep practicing, and soon you will be waking up after an exciting journey within the land of your dreams!

SNOOZE THE BLUES AWAY

Dreams provide us with an emotional outlet in which we can thoroughy understand our feelings and express our

Get a Grip

Professional golfer Jack Nicklaus's game went into a slump in the early 1960s. One night, he dreamed of swinging the club perfectly while using a different grip. The next time he played golf, he tried the grip from his dream. His game improved immediately, his scores soared, and he was out of his slump.

deepest emotions without fear of embarrassment. In dreams, we can experiment with new ideas or behaviors that we wouldn't normally dream of in real life.

Some people believe we use our dreams as a place of rehearsal to work out problems or make decisions by trying out different scenarios. By putting some intent into this process—for example, if we were to program a dream to rehearse a specific situation—we might shorten the time it would normally take to find a solution.

For instance, if you are having difficulty in a relationship, and a face-to-face discussion might result in hurt feelings, you could use your dreams as a testing ground for possible approaches. Incubate a dream in which you resolve the conflict for all parties involved. Program several dreams in order to try out various solutions. Sometimes our dreams will point out that we haven't been seeing someone or something in a realistic light.

Observe your behavior in your dreams. Do you handle situations in the same way you do when awake? Also notice the behaviors of your dream characters, as they may represent aspects of your own personality.

Using dreams to solve problems and provide advice can help you reduce stress in your everyday life. If you are feeling down, you can change your mood by having fun dream adventures or an uplifting, cheerful dream experience. Dreams give you a break from your daily routine and may give you a fresh, new outlook on life.

Dream On

The more you work and play with your dreams and the more familiar you become with your personal dream language, the more you will learn about your own personality. Your dreams are like a magic mirror, reflecting not only your outward appearance, but also showing you what lies within.

As you become aware of such things as why you make the choices that you do, how you approach conflict, or how your beliefs direct your thoughts and actions, you become more self-empowered. Being more self-empowered gives you the confidence to reach beyond your previous self-imposed boundaries.

Working with your dreams to enhance productivity or to experience nighttime adventures frees your creative spirit and allows it to grow and flourish. You may even discover talents and abilities you didn't know you possessed, which could open up a whole new world for you.

Take the time to look inside your dream world, and discover the treasures that lie within.

Definitions of Common Dream Symbols

Not all symbols have the same meanings for everyone. Use this dream dictionary as a basic guide to help interpret dreams.

The definitions in the following dream dictionary, especially those referred to as archetypes, are common to a large number of people. However, remember to think of each of the symbols within the context of the dream's environment. How a symbol appears is as important as the symbol itself. If any of the symbols evoke strong personal meanings or associations, then those are the correct meanings for you. After all, dreams are created by your dream self in your own dream language and are speaking to you. If a symbol in a dream has no strong personal meaning for you, check the dream dictionary for a general definition and determine if that meaning is appropriate to you. Rely on your intuition, and when you experience a feeling of recognition, you will know the definition is the right one for you.

ABBEY: An abbey suggests a place of solitude, peace of mind, and freedom from worries. *See also* Nun and Priest.

ABYSS: Looking into an abyss means someone is having relationship problems. Falling into an abyss may be a sign of depression and loneliness.

ACCIDENT: Someone is too self critical. *See also* Car.

ACCORDION: An accordion being played foretells festive times. If the accordion is silent, someone may be too busy to enjoy social activities. *See also* Music.

ACE: If an ace of hearts, a heart's desire will come true. If an ace of diamonds, it is a good omen for money matters. If an ace of clubs, expect success after a minor setback. If an ace of spades, watch out for disappointments. *See also* Cards and Solitaire.

ACORN: There is great potential for future development. *See also* Oak and Woods.

ACROBAT: Be flexible in dealings with business partners or in romantic relationships. *See also* Circus and Trapeze.

AEROBICS: If doing aerobics, someone has the ability to handle many situations at once. If watching others do aerobics, someone is procrastinating and work is piling up. *See also* Gym.

AFFAIR: A love affair in a dream is a good omen of a promising business relationship. *See also* Hug, Kiss, and Lap.

AIRPLANE: You may have high expectations of those around you and even higher expectations of yourself. *See also* Pilot and Wing.

AISLE: If someone walks down a church aisle, they will be involved in a love affair soon. To walk down other aisles indicates someone will reach their goals without distraction. *See also* Bell, Bride, Bridegroom, Church, and Reception.

ALCOHOL: Clouded thinking is distorting someone's perception and judgment. *See also* Thirst.

ALIEN: Is someone feeling alienated? Or is someone alienating someone else? *See also* Mars, Mercury, Moon, and Planets.

ALLIGATOR: A business project that has been slow to start may soon progress more quickly.

ALTAR: An altar suggests someone will receive good news, or it may be a play on words: Someone should plan to change *(alter)* their ways. *See also* Church, Nun, Preacher, and Priest.

AMBER: Anticipate a gift of money or real estate. *See also* Fossil and Gems.

AMBULANCE: Don't worry— help is on the way! *See also* Medicine.

AMETHYST: Amethysts imply peace and contentment in old age. *See also* Gems.

AMULET: Traditionally, an amulet is a sign of protection.

ANCHOR: Someone is firmly attached to ideas or convictions. If an anchor is being raised, it may be time to consider alternatives and set sail in a new direction. *See also* Ship.

ANGEL: An angel is a good omen indicating protection and security. The archetype is represented by spiritual ideals, a messenger of God, and wisdom of the inner self. *See also* Halo.

ANTIQUE: Valuable wisdom or advice is to be gained from an elder.

APARTMENT: Someone feels apart or separated from others and might want to do more socializing. *See also* House.

APPLAUSE: Someone may receive recognition and admiration for their talents. *See also* Theater.

APPLE: An apple signifies temptation. Someone should expect adverse consequences for giving in to temptation. *See also* Cider, Food, and Orchard.

APRON: Wearing an apron suggests domestic obligations have been neglected. More time should be spent with family. *See also* Housekeeper.

ARCH: To dream of walking under an arch predicts a happy marriage.

ARCHITECT: This is a sign that someone is more concerned with physical images and appearances than with inner beauty.

ARCTIC: Someone feels their life is dull and uneventful. They have not yet realized their potential. *See also* Ice, Iceberg, Icicles, and Snow.

ARMS: Arms are symbols of new ideas being welcomed and embraced. *See also* Bracelet, Elbow, and Hug.

ARROW: An arrow in flight is a good omen for romantic relationships. Be aware of to what or whom an arrow may be pointing. Follow the directions given. Take aim and go ahead as planned. *See also* Target.

ASHES: Ashes symbolize memories. They represent things burned or purged. They indicate that a situation is over. *See also* Burn, Fire, Firecrackers, Fireplace, Fireworks, and Smoke.

ASPEN TREE: Someone is displaying nervous behavior and should not be trusted. *See also* Leaf and Trees.

ATLAS: Looking at an atlas signifies an upcoming opportunity for a pleasure trip. *See also* Map.

ATTIC: An attic represents the mind, ideals (possibly lofty), and imagination. *See also* House.

AUDIENCE: Are you performing for an audience? Perhaps being yourself would be better. *See also* Stage and Theater.

BABY: A baby indicates a new beginning. It may also mean innocence, purity, or potential for growth. *See also* Birth, Cradle, Infant, Pregnant, Rattle, Triplets, and Twins.

BACK: What has someone turned their back on? Someone is unaware of, or is neglecting, something that is going on behind their back. *See also* Chiropractor and Spine.

BADGER: Is someone being badgered or pestered?

BAG: What burden is being carried? Someone is holding on to false hopes.

BAGPIPES: To see or hear bagpipes is a sign that assistance from an unexpected source may be received. The sound of bagpipes foreshadows an important event. *See also* Music.

BALCONY: To see a balcony in a dream portends romance and courtship. *See also* House.

BALL: The ball is in your court; take it and run with it! *See also* Bat, Hoop, Juggler, Pitch, Pitcher, Racket, Table Tennis, and Tennis.

BALLET: Keep on your toes! You may need to tread lightly around a situation or person. *See also* Dance.

BALLOONS: Celebrate! Happy and carefree days will follow.

BAMBOO: A bamboo indicates a strong will that can be flexible when necessary. *See also* Trees.

BANANA: A sign of prosperity and luck. A bunch of bananas indicates a small monetary windfall. *See also* Food and Orchard.

BANDAGE: A bandage suggests a temporary solution to a problem. *See also* Medicine.

BANJO: Someone might want to be careful where finances are concerned. A banjo

symbolizes monetary loss. *See also* Music.

BANK: A bank is a storehouse of riches. To dream of a bank is a good omen of financial security. *See also* Coins, Gold, Money, Penny, and Wealth.

BANQUET: Someone has everything they need. A banquet is a good omen for fortune and abundance. *See also* Food.

BARN: To dream of a barn full of animals symbolizes abundance. To dream of an empty barn implies that someone lacks nurturing. *See also* Farm and individual animal listings.

BASEMENT: Past emotional wounds are being ignored. It's time to face and release them. *See also* House.

BAT: To see flying bats denotes conflicting ideas and thoughts need sorting before

Foretelling the Future

One morning in 1966, a young schoolgirl named Eryl Mai told her mother about a dream she had just had in which she and others had gone to school, but the school was not there. "Something black had come down all over it," she explained. She then said, "I'm not afraid to die, Mommie. I'll be with Peter and June." Two days later, a slag deposit from the village coal mine slid down a mountain, killing 144 people. Three of those crushed under the slag were Eryl, Peter, and June.

any action should be taken. To dream of a baseball bat implies recreation and exercise would be good at this time. *See also* Ball, Pitch, and Pitcher.

BATH: A bath signifies cleansing, perhaps of unwanted situations or ideas. *See also* Bathroom, Bubbles, Towel, Tub, and Water.

BATHROOM: A bathroom is a symbol representing privacy and emotional cleansing. *See also* Bath, Bubbles, Shower, Toilet, Towel, and Tub.

BATTERY: Does someone need a boost? Batteries may need to be recharged. Take time out before tackling new projects.

BATTLE: A battle suggests an inner personal dilemma and a conflict of beliefs. *See also* Trench and Veteran.

BEACH: Someone deserves a vacation! *See also* Island, Ocean, Seashells, Vacation, and Water.

BEANS: Something thought to be worthwhile may turn out to be worthless. *See also* Food and String Beans.

BEAR: Someone's hidden talents may soon come out of hiding. If they do, it may happen under unusual circumstances.

BEAVER: Someone is working hard for what they want in a methodical, determined manner.

BED: It's time to rest! Someone needs a break from a busy lifestyle. *See also* Bedroom, Blanket, Pillow, and Quilt.

BEDROOM: A bedroom signifies privacy. Intimate thoughts are explored here. *See also* Bed, Blanket, Pillow, and Quilt.

BEEHIVE: A beehive is a place of activity and cooperative work. People are working toward a common goal and will be successful. *See also* Bees and Honey.

BEES: Expect a busy time ahead. If you hear bees buzzing, watch out for gossip. *See also* Beehive, Bugs, and Honey.

BEET: Someone is embarrassed due to a secret being revealed. *See also* Food.

BEGGAR: Someone may need to ask someone else for assistance, or someone shouldn't refuse help if it is offered. *See also* Hunger and Money.

BELL: A bell forecasts cheerful news. Wedding bells imply a union, either of business endeavors or personal relationships.

BELT: If fastened, a belt represents the completion of a cycle or phase. If unfastened, a belt implies that some restrictions need to be overcome before a project can be finished. *See also* Buckle.

BICYCLE: If someone is riding a bicycle, they will enjoy success from their own physical hard work. A bicycle by itself may denote travel, but the journey won't be too far away. *See also* Unicycle.

BINOCULARS: Examine what lies ahead, and bring things into focus.

BIRCH TREE: A birch tree symbolizes wisdom that comes with experience and age. *See also* Leaf and Trees.

BIRDS: Birds signify inspiration, messages, and ideas. A flock of birds can indicate many thoughts, sometimes confusing. *See also* Eggs, Feathers, Nest, Wing, and individual bird listings.

BIRTH: A birth is a new start in life. It represents fresh ideas. This is a good time to begin new projects. *See also* Baby and Pregnant.

BLACK: The color black symbolizes the unknown, mysteries, and secrets.

BLANKET: Something is or will be covered up and left unresolved unless action is taken. *See also* Bed, Bedroom, Picnic, Pillow, and Quilt.

BLIND: To be blind implies someone refuses to see something. To dream of a blind person means something is hidden. *See also* Eyes.

BLOSSOM: A blossom is a good omen of happiness and contentment. *See also* Bud, Flowers, Garden, Petal, and individual flower listings.

BLUE: The color blue represents devotion, loyalty, and confidence.

BONES: Bones can either mean someone should get down to the bare bones of a problem or circumstance will bring swift results. *See also* Fossil and Skeleton.

BOOK: Reading a book implies self-improvement through study and learning new skills. To see a book unopened indicates talents and abilities not yet used but available. *See also* Library, Page, and Paper.

BOOMERANG: Something thought to be thrown away may return. This could be a physical object, or it could be gossip.

BOOTS: Is someone getting the boot? If the boots are not on a person, it is a sign of rejection. If the boots are on a person or mannequin, someone is misusing their authority. *See also* Feet, Footprints, and Shoes.

BOTTLE: Don't bottle up emotions. Confide in someone trustworthy.

BOX: Does someone feel boxed in? An empty box can represent restricted or repressed emotions.

BRACELET: To wear a bracelet is a sign of a new friendship.

To lose a bracelet is a warning of an argument that could put strain on a friendship. *See also* Arms and Gems.

BRAKES: If the brakes are failing, someone feels out of control. If functioning, something may be stopped before it is completed. *See also* Car.

BRAMBLES: Are you in a thorny situation? You may suffer a few snags with a project. If you overtake brambles easily, your project may proceed with only minor problems. If you are caught in the brambles, you may need to do more work than expected in order to succeed.

BREAD: Bread portends an increase in income, a raise, or a bonus. *See also* Food.

BRICKS: Dreaming of bricks implies stubbornness and emotional blockages.

BRIDE: A new life adventure will soon begin. *See also* Aisle,

Bridegroom, Elopement, and Marriage.

BRIDEGROOM: A new business venture may prove profitable. *See also* Aisle, Bride, Elopement, and Marriage.

BRIDGE: If someone crosses a bridge, they will overcome difficulties. If a bridge is old and in need of repair, someone may have to work hard at achieving desired results, but they will succeed. If a bridge is new and strong, someone will succeed with ease.

BROCCOLI: Broccoli is a symbol of nutrition and healthy eating habits that should be followed. *See also* Cooking, Food, Garden, and Hunger.

BRONZE: Challenges have been met and overcome. Bronze is a good sign of progress and development. *See also* Medal.

BROOM: Make a clean sweep of things: Either physically clean your environs, or come clean in a relationship. *See also* Dust, Housekeeper, Mop, and Sweep.

BROTHER: The archetype is represented by the intellect and strength of character.

BROWN: The color brown symbolizes grounding, the earth, and family matters.

BUBBLES: Worries will quickly disappear. *See also* Bath, Bathroom, and Tub.

BUCKLE: If the buckle is damaged or broken, someone may be disappointed by a broken promise. *See also* Belt.

BUD: A new development may be a pleasant and welcome surprise. *See also* Blossom, Flowers, Garden, Petal, and individual flower listings.

BUGS: Something is bugging you. What is it? Bugs suggest small annoyances and inconveniences that will soon go away. *See also* individual bug listings.

BULL: Someone is stubborn and quick to anger. A white bull is an omen of very good luck.

BULLDOZER: An overbearing personality is making someone feel pressured to do something they would rather not do.

BURN: To burn something in a dream is a symbol of purging away unwanted emotions and beliefs. *See also* Ashes, Fire, and Smoke.

BUS: A bus designates the route your life is taking. Do you know where it's going? If you dream of bus stations, it may be time to decide on a new direction to take.

BUTTER: Is someone being buttered up? By whom? Why? *See also* Food.

BUTTERFLY: A butterfly implies transformation. Someone is entering a new phase of their life, one that might bring happiness and joy. *See also* Bugs.

BUTTONS: If someone loses a button in a dream, they should avoid extravagant purchases.

CABINETS: Unlooked-for help is right around the corner.

CAGE: Does someone feel caged? Why? A cage signifies inhibitions and restrictions.

CAKE: Have your cake, and eat it, too! A cake is a sign of forthcoming fulfillment and satisfaction. *See also* Food.

CALENDAR: Looking at a calendar predicts that you should set your schedule around an important event.

CAMEL: A camel is a sign of conservation and stored resources. When something is needed, it may be easy to obtain.

CAMP: A change of residence is possible in the near future. *See also* Tent.

CANDLE: A burning candle indicates a revelation or inspiration. An unlit candle warns of unfulfilled promises and disappointments. *See also* Chandelier and Wax.

CANE: Someone will receive unexpected support.

CANOE: If you are paddling the canoe, you enjoy self-reliance and independence. If the canoe is empty, perhaps it is a good time to get away by yourself. *See also* Oar and Water.

CAPTAIN: You are in control of your own destiny. Be clear about what you want, and go for it! *See also* Rigging, Sailor, and Ship.

CAR: A car represents the physical body. A car in good running order implies a healthy body, whereas a car in need of repair implies that someone may need a medical checkup. *See also* Accident, Brakes, Detour, Jack, Limousine, Mechanic, Park, Passenger, Seatbelt, Traffic, Truck, and U-Turn.

CARDS: Playing cards indicate gambles in life. Take a chance, and expect a fortunate outcome. *See also* Ace, Joker, and Solitaire.

CARNATIONS: It could be a play on words, as in *reincarnation*. Has something or someone reentered your life lately? *See also* Flowers.

CAROL: Hearing carols is a prediction of a prosperous and happy year ahead. *See also* Music and Sing.

CARROT: Someone is being tempted by an alluring offer. *See also* Food.

CARTOON: Someone may be experiencing feelings of embarrassment and foolishness due to a minor misunderstanding. *See also* Television.

CASTLE: A castle is a good sign of a happy marriage and family life. *See also* Joker, King, Knight, Palace, Prince, Princess, and Queen.

CAT: A cat is a symbol of self-reliance and independence. *See also* Kitten.

CATALOG: Many options and opportunities are available at this time. Choose carefully, keeping priorities in mind.

CATTLE: Cattle indicate contentment and peacefulness. If someone is driving cattle, they are bringing all their resources together. *See*

A Dream With a Twist

Chemist Fredrich von Kekule, experiencing difficulty determining the molecular structure of benzene, fell asleep and dreamed of atoms in long chains, swirling and twisting in a snakelike fashion. Suddenly, one of the "snakes" bit its own tail and whirled before his eyes. When he awoke, he made the groundbreaking realization that the benzene molecule is ringlike.

also Cow, Fields, Pasture, and Ranch.

CAULIFLOWER: Someone may receive a small gift of thanks for an appreciated favor. *See also* Food.

CAVE: If someone is inside a cave, they may be hiding from certain issues. If someone is emerging from a cave, they may have or may soon overcome difficulties.

CEILING: Someone may meet with limitations; another approach to a situation may be sought.

CELEBRITY: A celebrity is a sign of success and fame. Someone may do very well in their endeavors. *See also* Television.

CELERY: Someone doesn't fit in with the crowd. Find a more suitable group to join. *See also* Food.

CEMETERY: A problem will be laid to rest. *See also* Death and Pallbearer.

CENTIPEDE: A centipede is an unfavorable omen for business, but troubles may not be long-lived. *See also* Bugs.

CHAIN: A chain is a link, a connecting factor. To dream someone is bound in chains indicates they feel held back in something they want to do or accomplish. What is it?

CHAIR: A chair represents someone's position in the workplace. If empty, a new position may be available. If occupied, there may be changes made in the workplace. *See also* Table.

CHAMELEON: Someone is not being true to themselves, or something may not be what it appears to be at first glance.

CHANDELIER: A lit chandelier is a good omen for social success. An unlit chandelier means it may take some time before new ideas or concepts are accepted. To dream of swinging from a chandelier is a sign of luck and happiness. *See also* Candle and Wax.

CHERRIES: Cherries foretell temptations in love and romance. *See also* Food.

CHERRY TREE: To see a cherry tree in a dream indicates someone is not being entirely honest. *See also* Cherries, Food, and Trees.

CHICKENS: Don't count the chickens before they hatch! Curb impulsive behavior. *See also* Birds, Food, and Rooster.

CHIROPRACTOR: To dream of a chiropractor means something is out of alignment and needs adjusting. If the chiropractor is working on a patient, it is a sign that emotions are out of balance. *See also* Back and Spine.

CHOCOLATE: Indulge and pamper yourself. You deserve it! *See also* Food.

CHOKE: Choking indicates that you are having difficulty expressing yourself.

CHURCH: A church represents spiritual beliefs. If the church is empty, someone is seeking answers. If full, someone enjoys a satisfying spiritual life. *See also* Aisle, Altar, Nun, Preacher, Priest, and Temple.

CIDER: Cider is a symbol of good luck. If someone drinks it, their luck is increased. *See also* Apple and Thirst.

CIGARETTE: A cigarette is a symbol of addiction and of habits that are hard to break. More discipline is required.

CIRCLES: Is someone going in circles? Stop and take another look at what is happening before continuing.

CIRCUS: Is life like a three-ring circus? A circus is a sign to slow down and take on fewer responsibilities or finish one project at a time. *See also* Acrobat, Clown, and Trapeze.

CLAM: Clam up! Someone may want to keep quiet about someone else's personal problems. Discretion may be appreciated. *See also* Food.

CLAW: Someone feels threatened or is jealous of someone else and holds too tight to these feelings.

CLAY: A situation can be changed for the better with a simple change in attitude.

CLIFF: To see a cliff is a sign of an upcoming challenge. To jump off a cliff indicates that someone may make a big change in their life. To be pushed off a cliff is a sign that someone may do something unwillingly for someone else.

CLOAK: If someone is wearing a cloak, they are concealing something from others. To see a cloak is a warning that an unpleasant situation is coming, but those involved may be protected.

CLOCK: Time is of the essence.

CLOSET: An empty closet denotes loss. A full closet is a sign of a happy future.

CLOUD: Peacefulness is represented by soft, fluffy clouds. A dark cloud can represent depression or worry. *See also* Fog, Hail, Lightning, Rain, Rainbow, Sky, Storm, and Thunder.

CLOVER: A clover is a lucky symbol, particularly if it is a four-leaf clover. *See also* Leaf.

CLOWN: Either things are not being taken seriously, or someone may need to take things less seriously and enjoy themselves more. *See also* Circus and Parade.

CLUTTER: Things may be getting out of hand. Get back in control, and bring order to the chaos.

COAT: Something is being covered up. What is it? Why?

COBWEB: Let go of muddled thoughts in order to make a decision. *See also* Spider.

COINS: If someone is given coins, they can expect profit and gain, perhaps through a raise or successful investment. If someone finds coins, it means good luck can be expected with new investments. *See also* Bank, Jackpot, Money, and Penny.

COLLAR: A dog collar implies that someone is being led into a situation because of someone else's influence. They should question if they really want to be led before going any further.

COMPUTER: A computer is a symbol of communication, programming, and one's thoughts. Positive and productive thoughts create positive experiences.

CONTEST: To dream of winning a contest implies that someone desires recognition. To dream of losing a contest is an indication that someone has competition in the workplace.

CONVENT: To enter a convent represents going within to explore one's spirituality. To see a convent represents a restriction being imposed on someone. *See also* Nun.

COOKING: Plans are being cooked up. *See also* Feast, Food, Oven, Recipe, Stove, and individual food listings.

CORNER: To face a corner is a warning that someone may receive a reprimand. To have one's back to a corner represents a limiting or restricting situation. To turn a street corner foretells of a pleasant surprise.

COTTON: False flattery will be used to gain your favor. Don't accept it if you are not comfortable with a request.

COUCH: Someone has a hidden agenda. Make sure

everything is out in the open before signing any legal documents.

COURTHOUSE: Someone feels they must justify their actions or intent. *See also* Judge, Jury, and Lawyer.

COW: To dream of a cow in a field is a sign of domestic comfort and nurturing. A cow in a barn is a sign of hard work to come, but the rewards may be great. *See also* Cattle, Fields, Milk, Pasture, and Ranch.

COYOTE: Beware of a sly person where relationships are concerned.

CRADLE: An empty cradle represents unfulfilled wishes. A baby in a cradle implies fulfillment in the future. *See also* Baby.

CREAM: Cream implies the cream of the crop and the best possible outcome of a situation. *See also* Food and Milk.

CREDIT CARD: Someone has the means to do as they please for a while; eventually they may have to pay up.

CROSSROADS: Is someone at a crossroads in life? Crossroads denote a time of decision and self-reflection. *See also* Path.

CROW: Someone is boasting about their achievements. *See also* Birds.

CROWN: A crown is a sign of respect and authority. If you dream of wearing a crown, you have earned the respect of your peers. *See also* King and Prince.

CRUTCH: A crutch is a means of support. Someone may be supported during a time of need.

CRY: To cry in a dream is a sign of an emotional release. To see someone crying is an omen of sad news. To hear a baby cry is sign of good news.

CURTAIN: If the curtains are closed, there is more to a story than what has been told. If the curtains are open, there is an opportunity for advancement in the work-place. *See also* Window.

DAISY: A daisy signifies kind-ness and affection. Wishes are coming true. *See also* Blossom, Flowers, Garden, Leaf, and Petal.

DAM: A dam suggests locked or repressed emotions. *See also* Water.

DANCE: If you are dancing, you may be dancing around issues. If others dance, you will soon be meeting new friends and engaging in more social events. *See also* Ballet, Jig, and Tango.

DANDELION: If there is a field of dandelions, someone will hear news of a forthcoming wedding of a close friend. If someone is gathering dande-lions, there will be word of a marriage breaking up. *See also* Flowers and Weeds.

DARTS: Playing darts indicates someone is focused on a target and may achieve their goal successfully and swiftly.

DAWN: An innovative idea or solution will dawn on you.

DEAF: If you are deaf, you are not listening to some-thing. If someone else is deaf, your words are falling on deaf ears: Either speak to someone else, or find a way to get your point across.

DEATH: Death marks the end of a stage in life and a time of great change. *See also* Ceme-tery, Pallbearer, and Widow.

DEN: A den is an indication that it's now time for contemplation and self-reflection.

DENTIST: Someone needs to be sure of the facts before

One Dream Saves Millions

Canadian physician Frederick Banting had a dream that led to a breakthrough in diabetes research. One night he woke from a dream and wrote down three lines of instructions for an experimental procedure. Banting and his colleagues performed the experiment and, as a result, discovered insulin.

speaking out. A dentist represents a clear conscience as well as a clean mouth. *See also* False Teeth, Mouth, Tongue, and Tooth.

DESERT: A desert is an indication of a period of loneliness that will soon pass. *See also* Oasis.

DETOUR: To take a detour represents a career change. To see a detour sign means someone is on the wrong track. *See also* Car.

DEVIL: The archetype is represented by negative aspects of the self.

DEW: Dew is a favorable sign of encouragement and hope. *See also* Water.

DIAMOND: The gem suggests outstanding debts may be paid faster than expected. The shape represents a union of opposites. *See also* Gems.

DIARY: A diary denotes thoughts and memories of the past. *See also* Ink, Page, Paper, and Writing.

DIET: Someone may need to cut back on expenses. *See also* Food and Hunger.

DINING ROOM: A dining room symbolizes sustenance and nurturing.

DINOSAUR: Old and outdated ideas are holding someone back. Be more open to new experiences and opinions. *See also* Bones and Fossil.

DIPLOMA: Someone has successfully overcome a problem. Congratulations! *See also* Graduation.

DISGUISE: Something is hidden. *See also* Mask.

DITCH: Either protective barriers are in place, or something you have been holding onto should be ditched. *See also* Trench.

DOCTOR: A doctor is a symbol of healing where the body is concerned and a sign that things are being resolved where relationships are concerned. *See also* Medicine and Nurse.

DOG: A dog represents unconditional love, loyalty, and obedience.

DOLL: Someone has an idealized concept of someone else. There is more to that person than appearances indicate. *See also* Dollhouse.

DOLLHOUSE: Someone is not being realistic when it comes to a family matter. *See also* Doll.

DOLPHIN: A dolphin symbolizes a sudden release of tension and feelings of freedom.

DOME: A dome indicates recognition of your achievements.

DONKEY: Someone has many burdens, but they can carry their burdens if they take enough time.

DOOR: An open door is a sign of new opportunities. A closed door means an opportunity is no longer available; move on to something else. *See also* Doormat and Hinge.

DOORMAT: Does someone feel like a doormat? They should stand up for themselves and voice their opinions. *See also* Door.

DOVE: A dove represents happiness in the home. *See also* Birds.

DRAGON: A dragon is a symbol of force and power. It is a good omen for those on a spiritual quest.

DRAGONFLY: Someone may be invited to go on a short but very enjoyable journey. *See also* Bugs.

DRESS: An indication that carefree days are ahead. Enjoy!

DROUGHT: A drought predicts a period of loss, followed by a great relief. *See also* Water.

DROWNING: Is someone in over their head? Dreaming about drowning indicates overwhelming emotions and stress. *See also* Swim, Underwater, and Water.

DRUM: Dance to the beat of your own drum. Follow your heart. *See also* Music.

DUCK: Is someone ducking responsibilities? They may face challenging and awkward situations head on. *See also* Birds and Food.

DUEL: A duel implies confrontation and arguments. *See also* Quarrel.

DUST: Something has been neglected. *See also* Broom, Housekeeper, Mop, Sweep, and Vacuum Cleaner.

EARRINGS: Harmless flirtation may be enjoyed in a social setting. *See also* Ears and Gems.

EARS: Someone is open to new ideas and to trying new things. *See also* Earrings and Hearing Aid.

EARTHQUAKE: Is someone on shaky ground? Or do things need to be shaken up in order to move on?

EAVESDROP: If someone is eavesdropping in a dream,

they might want to beware of half-truths and gossip. Don't rely on secondhand information.

ECHO: Someone's words are being repeated. They should be careful of what they say.

ECLIPSE: Something is obscured from view. Wait until it can be seen more clearly. *See also* Moon, Sky, and Sun.

EEL: A golden opportunity could slip through someone's fingers if not acted upon immediately.

EGGS: Eggs predict financial success over time, like a nest egg. *See also* Birds, Eggshells, Food, Nest, and Yolk.

EGGSHELLS: Someone may feel fragile and be withdrawing into their "shell." If the shells are broken, someone may have recently overcome difficult circumstances. *See also* Eggs.

ELBOW: Someone is bending to the will of another. It's time to set some boundaries. *See also* Arms.

ELECTION: Someone will either be asked to take on more responsibilities or experience a rise in status.

ELECTRICIAN: To dream of an electrician is a sign that someone's energy and drive are at a low ebb and need a boost. *See also* Electricity.

ELECTRICITY: Electricity signifies a surge of energy. It implies creative, powerful ideas. *See also* Electrician and Static.

ELEPHANT: Elephants represent memories. (As the adage goes: Elephants never forget.)

ELEVATOR: If someone is riding upward in an elevator, it is a good sign. If someone is descending, it is an unfavorable sign.

ELOPEMENT: To dream that you are eloping predicts a long and happy marriage. To dream of someone else eloping represents impulsive decisions that are not always favorable. *See also* Bride and Bridegroom.

EMERALD: There may be some legal concerns regarding an inheritance. *See also* Gems.

ENAMEL: Something has been glossed over. Review recent circumstances to see what has been passed over or missed. *See also* Paint.

ENCYCLOPEDIA: An encyclopedia is a source of knowledge. It represents wisdom gained through the written word as opposed to wisdom gained through experience. *See also* Book and Library.

ENGINE: An engine indicates a driving force. Someone can push forward and succeed.

EXPLOSION: A sudden outburst may surprise you. *See also* Torpedo.

EYEBROWS: Thick, bushy eyebrows denote respect and esteem. Arched eyebrows suggest a forthcoming surprise.

EYEGLASSES: If you aren't wearing glasses (and you normally do), you are not seeing something clearly. If you are wearing glasses (and you normally don't), you will be shown insight into a problem. *See also* Eyes.

EYELASHES: Something is alluring but is of little value. It would be wise to pass it up. *See also* Eyes.

EYES: If the eyes are open, they are signs of clarity. If closed, someone is refusing to see a situation as it really is. *See also* Blind, Eyeglasses, and Eyelashes.

FACTORY: A factory signifies routine, repetitive actions and a need for change.

FAIRY: Someone's wishes will come true when least expected.

FALSE TEETH: Don't form opinions based upon information from an unreliable source. Double-check the facts. *See also* Dentist and Mouth.

FAN: To fan yourself indicates an embarrassing situation will soon pass or you are too intense about something— cool it!

FARM: If well kept, a farm indicates good health and prosperity. If run down, some important legal issues need attending to. *See also* Barn and individual animal listings.

FATHER: The archetype is represented by a masculine authority figure and the provider.

FEAST: A feast represents success and rewards. *See also* Cooking and Food.

FEATHERS: Feathers suggest luxury and glamour. Floating feathers signify celebration and fulfilled wishes. *See also* Birds.

FEET: Feet symbolize support and independence. *See also* Boots, Footprints, and Shoes.

FEMALE: The archetype is represented by nurturing qualities, fertility, intuition, and emotions.

FENCE: A fence points to limitations. If someone is climbing over a fence, it shows that they have exceeded prior limitations. *See also* Gate and Picket.

FERRET: With perseverance, someone will discover what they need to know.

FIDDLE: To see a fiddle is a sign that someone is being

dishonest. To hear fiddle music foretells of family reunions and celebrations. *See also* Music and Violin.

FIELDS: If untended fields, someone has work ahead of them. If full of crops, someone will be rewarded for their efforts. *See also* Grain, Horse, Oats, Pasture, and individual animal listings.

FIRE: Fire implies passion, temper, and emotions. If it is smoldering, someone is repressing emotions. If ablaze, things may be getting out of control. If someone puts out a fire, they are cooling tempers. *See also* Ashes, Burn, Firecrackers, Fire Escape, Firehouse, Fireplace, Fireworks, Smoke, and Torch.

FIRECRACKERS: Petty irritations will stop soon. *See also* Ashes, Fire, Fireworks, and Smoke.

FIRE ESCAPE: A fire escape predicts a way out of a difficult situation. *See also* Fire.

FIREFLIES: Fireflies are indications of happy, comforting childhood memories. *See also* Bugs.

FIREHOUSE: Someone is in control of their fiery emotions. *See also* Fire.

FIREPLACE: A fireplace is a sign of comfort and content-ment in family affairs. *See also* Ashes, Fire, and Smoke.

FIREWORKS: Fireworks suggest cause for celebration. Anticipate excitement and joy. *See also* Ashes, Fire, Firecrackers, and Smoke.

FISH: To dream of catching a fish predicts profit and gain. To dream of going fishing implies someone is searching for information. *See also* Net and Water.

Prophetic President

While sleeping in the White House, President Abraham Lincoln dreamed that he could hear muffled noises, like sobbing. He got out of bed and went to search for the source of the sounds. When he entered the East Room, he found many people gathered around a coffin on a raised platform, guarded by soldiers. The face of the body in the coffin was covered. Lincoln asked one of the guards, "Who is dead in the White House?" The soldier answered, "The President. He was killed by an assassin." About two weeks after this dream, President Abraham Lincoln was assassinated by John Wilkes Booth. After his death, his coffin lay on a platform in the East Room of the White House, guarded by soldiers.

FLOOD: Does someone feel caught in the tide of overwhelming emotions? Why? *See also* Water.

FLOOR: A floor is a sign of stability. Someone's ideas are on solid ground.

FLOUR: Baking with flour is a good omen for long-term financial investments. An unopened sack of flour is a sign of unused potential. *See also* Food.

FLOWERS: Someone will receive a gift of gratitude and recognition. *See also* Blossom, Bud, Garden, Leaf, Petal, Seeds, Thorn, and individual flower listings.

FLUTE: Someone is about to embark on a new path in the workforce. *See also* Music.

FOG: Things are unclear at this time. If the fog is on land, a personal relationship is troubled by lack of communication. If it is at sea or over water, there is emotional confusion. If it is lifting, someone will achieve clarity. *See also* Cloud.

FOOD: Food is a representation of sustenance, a necessity of survival. If someone is eating, they are receiving necessary input. If someone is preparing or serving food, they are feeding a problem; withdrawing energy may help the problem go away more quickly. *See also* Cooking, Diet, Feast, Fork, Freezer, Hunger, Kitchen, Napkin, Plate, Refrigerator, Spoon, Thirst, and individual food listings.

FOOL: The archetype is represented by self-sabotage, obstacles, and the part of us that holds us back from accomplishing our goals.

FOOTPRINTS: Is someone walking in someone else's footprints? Perhaps they should follow their own path.

See also Boots, Feet, and Shoes.

FORGET-ME-NOT: A forget-me-not could be a figure of speech: Someone wants your attention. *See also* Flowers.

FORK: This could mean a fork in the road, a time of decision. The choice will impact the future; decide carefully. *See also* Food, Napkin, Path, Plate, and Spoon.

FOSSIL: Something seems set in stone. A fossil suggests old, rigid beliefs.

FOUNDATION: To dream of a building's foundation implies a stable financial future.

FOUNTAIN: A fountain implies abundance and refreshment. *See also* Water.

FOX: A fox is representative of a crafty person.

FRECKLES: Freckles denote attraction to another person.

FREEZER: To put something in a freezer indicates someone is putting off something that should be dealt with immediately. *See also* Food, Kitchen, Refrigerator, and individual food listings.

FROGS: Frogs are very good omens for happiness in love, business, and/or family matters.

FUDGE: Are you cheating someone or yourself? Being honest will allow for few repercussions. *See also* Food.

GARAGE: A garage is a sign of protection and security. *See also* House.

GARBAGE: A situation needs cleaning up. Work through emotional reactions, and get to the core of the matter. *See also* Junk and Recycle.

GARDEN: A garden symbolizes the dreamer's environment and fruits of labor. A thriving garden predicts prosperity and abundance in love and money. *See also* Blossom, Bud, Flowers, Herbs, Root, Seeds, Weeds, and individual flower and vegetable listings.

GARLIC: To smell garlic is a sign of an argument to come. To see garlic indicates there is a conflict that needs to be resolved. *See also* Food.

GARNET: Affairs of the heart are a priority now. *See also* Gems.

GATE: If someone passes through an open gate, they will accomplish their goals easily. If they find a gate closed, they will be hampered by details before they can proceed. *See also* Fence, Hinge, and Picket.

GEMS: Gems indicate riches and inspirations. *See also* Bracelet, Earrings, Necklace, Ring, Treasure, and individual gem listings.

GIANT: A giant represents insecurity. You may be feeling inferior to someone, or you may be seeing things out of proportion. If you are the giant, you may be over-whelming someone.

GIFT: To be presented with a gift suggests the awakening of unused talents or skills. To give a gift means that someone may help another realize their potential.

GIRAFFE: A giraffe implies feelings of arrogance and superiority. Someone is looking down on others.

GLACIER: A glacier suggests feelings of oppression and of being overwhelmed. *See also* Ice.

GLOVE: To wear gloves is a sign of distancing one's self from others. To remove gloves indicates that someone is ready for a new challenge. *See also* Hands.

GLUE: Glue signifies a sticky situation that should be handled with tact and discretion.

GOAT: A goat symbolizes physical energy, determination, and prosperity.

GOD: The archetype is represented by a creator, masculine dominance, power, and control of destiny.

GODDESS: The archetype is represented by feminine dominance, power, and control of destiny.

GOLD: Gold is a symbol denoting perfection and the highest awards. *See also* Bank, Medal, Money, Nugget, Pan, Rainbow, and Treasure.

GOOSE: Is someone being a silly goose? A goose signifies frivolity and humor. *See also* Birds and Food.

GOWN: A gown is a symbol of formality and proper behavior.

GRADUATION: A graduation points to a time of transition. *See also* Diploma.

GRAIN: Grain is an omen of rewards from effort and determination. *See also* Fields, Pasture, and Silo.

GRANDPARENTS: The archetypes are represented by wisdom that comes with age and experience.

GRAPES: Grapes represent abundance and satisfaction. *See also* Food and Raisins.

GRASSHOPPER: Either someone has jumped to a conclusion, or something may proceed in short bursts of activity. *See also* Bugs.

GRAY: The color gray represents a transitional period where things are not yet clearly defined.

GREEN: The color green symbolizes growth, renewal, and abundance.

GUITAR: To hear a guitar being played means that there are favorable things happening behind the scenes. A pleasant surprise awaits! *See also* Music.

GURU: An acquaintance or friend may provide you with excellent advice.

GYM: A gym is a symbol of self-discipline. If working out, someone is exercising self-discipline. If the gym is empty, more discipline is required. *See also* Aerobics.

HAIL: A seemingly unfavorable situation or event will turn out to be very fortunate. *See also* Cloud, Rain, Sky, and Water.

HAIR: Hair signifies energy and strength. If hair is clean and well-kept, the person has good health. If hair is unhealthy or unkempt, the person needs to regain their energy. To comb hair means someone is putting positive effort into a relationship or project. *See also* Hairdresser, Head, and Wig.

HAIRDRESSER: Someone is unsatisfied with their image and wants to make changes. *See also* Hair.

HALLWAY: Someone may make favorable contacts in the near future.

HALO: A halo represents purity and goodness. *See also* Angel.

HAMMER: A hammer indicates determination and strength. Hammer home a few points before words will take effect. *See also* Nail.

HAMPER: A laundry hamper indicates someone will be hampered by obstacles, but they will not affect the final outcome. *See also* Laundry.

HANDS: If empty, someone may receive aid. If full, some-

one is able to handle hard situations well. *See also* Glove.

HARBOR: A harbor is a port in the storm. It is a place to rest and regroup away from the storm. A harbor could also mean the thoughts you are harboring. *See also* Ship and Water.

HAT: A hat is indicative of your role in life. For example, if you wear a police officer's hat, you may be enforcing your ideas of right and wrong upon someone else. If you wear a nurse's cap, you may be nurturing someone.

HAWK: Someone may be rewarded for their keen observations. *See also* Birds.

HAYSTACK: A seemingly overwhelming situation may turn out to be favorable. *See also* Fields.

HEAD: If seen from the front, someone is heading in the

right direction. If the back of the head is seen, someone is heading in the wrong direction. *See also* Hair.

HEARING AID: Someone may experience a disagreement due to a lack of communication; wait until tempers cool before trying to resolve the dispute. *See also* Ears.

HEART: Someone needs to get to the heart of the matter.

HEATHER: Heather, especially white heather, is a symbol of good fortune. *See also* Flowers.

HEIRLOOM: Someone will soon receive a special gift from a family member.

HELICOPTER: It is better to get a view of the big picture before making any commitments. *See also* Pilot.

HERBS: Herbs suggest health and healing. *See also* Food.

HERMIT: Someone would benefit from being alone. Someone should reflect upon life and goals before continuing along the path. *See also* House.

HERO: The archetype is represented by the rescuer, salvation, and the part of us that can handle crisis.

HERON: A situation calls for grace, poise, and silence. Keep thoughts to yourself until all sides of the story are heard. *See also* Birds.

HIGH HEELS: If wearing high heels, someone is trying to impress another. If the high heels are on display, someone is interested in attracting a new romance.

HILL: A hill points to goals and ambitions. If someone is at the hill's bottom, their goal is in sight, but they must work to attain it. If someone stands on a hilltop, they have

The Association for the Study of Dreams

The Association for the Study of Dreams (ASD) is an international nonprofit organization created to promote awareness of dreams and to encourage dream research. Each year, ASD holds a five-day conference. Everyone from professional sleep and dream researchers, psychologists, and scientists to the general public are welcome to attend and participate. Anyone interested in dreams can join ASD. For further information, check out the ASD Web site (www.asdreams.org).

reached their goal and can enjoy a position of security. If someone comes down a hill or the hill is behind them, they have overcome an obstacle, and the way ahead is clear. *See also* Mountain.

HINGE: The outcome of one thing depends upon the success of another. Some preliminary preparations may be required before embarking on a new endeavor. *See also* Door and Gate.

HIPPOPOTAMUS: A hippo suggests a period of boredom followed by a burst of activity.

HOBBY: To pursue a hobby in a dream is a good sign that a period of relaxation is at hand. Enjoy the time off!

HOLE: Watch out for traps!

HOLLY: A prickly situation is at hand. Proceed with caution and discretion.

HONEY: Honey implies sweetness and love in the home. It is a very lucky sign. *See also* Beehive, Bees, and Food.

HOOP: Someone may need to jump through a few hoops before they reach their desired goal. *See also* Ball.

HORN: An animal horn denotes sexual prowess. A musical horn signals either news or an event. If someone is blowing a horn, they will enjoy success. *See also* Music and Ram.

HORSE: A horse is a sign of energy, of horsepower. If someone is riding a horse, they are in control of their destiny. *See also* Fields, Horseshoe, Lasso, Oats, Pasture, Ranch, Riding, and Saddle.

HORSESHOE: Traditionally, a horseshoe signifies good luck and fortune. If someone is shoeing a horse, their luck will come as a result of their own efforts. *See also* Horse.

HOTEL: Someone is in a transitional phase. A period of rest may soon be followed by a burst of activity.

HOURGLASS: An hourglass indicates a sense of urgency. Time is running out!

HOUSE: A house symbolizes the self. Its appearance represents the self-image of the dreamer. For example, if the house is gleaming clean with everything in its place, the dreamer may be a perfectionist. If the house is untidy and cluttered, the dreamer may be easily distracted. *See also* Apartment, Balcony, Hermit, Hut, Mansion, Patio, Penthouse, Porch, Rafters, Roof, Trailer, Yard, and individual room listings.

HOUSEKEEPER: If the housekeeper works for you, people are working behind the scenes in your favor. If you are the housekeeper, you may be taking on someone else's responsibilities. *See also* Apron, Broom, Dust, Mop, Sweep, Vacuum Cleaner, and Varnish.

HUG: Expect a visit from someone you haven't seen in a while. *See also* Arms.

HUMMING: To hear humming in a dream is a good omen. An important message may make a lot of people happy. *See also* Music.

HUMMINGBIRD: A hummingbird is a symbol of diligence and perseverance. *See also* Birds.

HUNGER: Hunger denotes an intense desire for something lacking or absent. *See also* Beggar, Diet, Food, and individual food listings.

HURRICANE: A hurricane predicts arguments, anger, and upheaval. *See also* Storm.

HUT: A hut marks the simple things in life, the basic necessities. *See also* House.

ICE: Ice is a symbol of rigid, cool behavior. It indicates a lack of feeling. *See also* Arctic, Glacier, Iceberg, Icicles, and Snow.

ICEBERG: Be aware that there is more to a situation or person than meets the eye. *See also* Arctic, Ice, Icicles, and Snow.

ICICLES: Soon troubles will melt away. If icicles are dripping, problems will dissolve quickly. *See also* Arctic, Ice, Iceberg, and Snow.

IDOL: Someone may discover a secret but not reveal it to anyone else.

IMPOSTER: Either you aren't being true to yourself, or someone is not being honest with you.

INCENSE: Incense is a symbol of spiritual searching. *See also* Odor.

INFANT: The archetype is represented by innocence, purity, and beginnings. *See also* Baby.

INK: Read the fine print in all business and legal transactions. *See also* Diary, Letter, Page, Paper, Quill, and Writing.

INTERRUPTIONS: Dreaming of being interrupted while you are speaking predicts upsets in love relationships.

INTERVIEW: To conduct an interview is a sign that someone is questioning their abilities. To be interviewed means that someone is about to make a lifestyle change.

INVISIBILITY: Invisibility represents things unseen. If you are invisible, you may be feeling overlooked or neglected. If someone else is invisible, you may have been taking them for granted.

IRON: An iron is an implication of willpower. Ironing is a good sign that someone will work out difficulties at their own pace.

ISLAND: An island indicates solitude and isolation. If surrounded by peaceful waters, it is a good time to be alone. If surrounded by rough waters, perhaps it would be better to get help rather than tackle a problem alone. *See also* Beach and Water.

ITCH: Someone has been dwelling too much on small annoyances lately. Ignoring the annoyances will force them to resolve themselves.

IVY: Ivy denotes clingy or needy friends. Also, an ideal or something from the past could be being held onto when it should be let go. *See also* Leaf.

JACK: A mechanical jack indicates relief from burdens. *See also* Car.

JACKET: A jacket is a sign that personal matters are being covered up.

JACKPOT: If you win a jackpot, you can expect an

exciting surprise. If someone else wins it, you will obtain something you want with little or no effort. *See also* Coins, Money, and Wealth.

JADE: Jade suggests financial gain and prosperity. It is a good omen for money matters. *See also* Gems.

JAM: Jam means delays, like traffic jams. Have patience—things will work out eventually. If you dream of eating jam, it signifies domestic contentment. *See also* Food, Preserves, and individual fruit listings.

JASMINE: To smell jasmine in a dream predicts a new romance. To see jasmine implies harmony in a relationship. *See also* Flowers and Odor.

JASPER: Someone is upset about a situation and needs to take a closer look at details before a resolution can be sought. *See also* Gems.

JAYWALK: Daydreams and fantasies are distracting someone from their work.

JELLYFISH: A jellyfish is a spineless creature. You may be overly sensitive and cowardly when it comes to standing up for yourself. More self-assertiveness is needed.

JIG: To dance a jig predicts celebration, possibly of a forthcoming marriage. *See also* Dance.

JOKER: Don't be fooled by someone's supposedly naive behavior. *See also* Cards, Castle, and Palace.

JOURNEY: A journey is either a symbol of someone's path in life or a prediction of a long trip. *See also* Luggage, Passport, Pilgrimage, Pioneer, and Quest.

JUDGE: If you dream of a judge, reexamine the circumstances surrounding an issue carefully before making a decision. If you dream of being judged, it indicates you feel guilty about something. *See also* Courthouse, Jury, and Lawyer.

JUG: If the jug is full, you have many good friendships. If you are drinking from a jug, you enjoy good health. *See also* Thirst and individual beverage listings.

JUGGLER: Does someone have too many balls in the air? It may be necessary to rearrange a schedule. *See also* Ball.

JUMP: Someone will over-come obstacles in their path.

JUNGLE: Don't get entangled in someone else's affairs.

JUNK: Let go of unwanted thoughts or ideas. *See also* Garbage and Recycle.

JURY: Does someone feel like they are on trial? A jury suggests feelings of defen-siveness. *See also* Courthouse, Judge, and Lawyer.

KANGAROO: A kangaroo symbolizes restlessness, movement from place to place or from relationship to relationship.

KELP: Don't get entangled in someone else's affairs. Maintain a neutral position.

KETTLE: A kettle denotes family matters. If it is steam-ing, expect pleasant news. *See also* Tea, Thirst, and Water.

KEY: Someone has what they need to proceed with a plan or to solve a problem. If someone has lost their key, they are missing something needed to complete a project. If someone is given a key, they will receive assistance from a friend or associate. *See also* Lock.

KING: The archetype is represented by lawfulness,

leadership, authority, and justice. *See also* Castle, Crown, Palace, and Throne.

KISS: A kiss is a sign of affection, warmth, and intimacy. To receive a kiss means a pleasant surprise is coming. To give a kiss signifies someone may confide their secrets to another. *See also* Affair and Hug.

KITCHEN: A kitchen symbolizes plans and preparations. *See also* Food, Freezer, Kitchen Sink, Oven, Refrigerator, and Stove.

KITCHEN SINK: Someone is overwhelmed by too many unimportant personal issues. It's time to set priorities. *See also* Kitchen.

KITE: A kite implies high hopes. If someone flies a kite easily, they can expect their plans to work out favorably. If the string breaks or the kite fails to catch the wind, they should expect delays.

KITTEN: A kitten is a sign of a playful person or a brief romantic encounter. *See also* Cat.

KNEE: A knee is a sign of humility and respect for authority. *See also* Legs.

KNEEL: If you are kneeling, you have respect for others. If others are kneeling, you have earned their respect.

KNIGHT: Someone will be rescued from a distressing situation or conflict. *See also* Castle and Palace.

KNIT: Knitting indicates a reunion either of family or close friends. It may also mean healing energies. *See also* Needle and Sewing.

KNOT: Knots signify problems that need unraveling. If someone is tying knots, they are creating problems.

Gifts of the Goddess

Indian mathematical genius Srinivasa Ramanujan was noted for his uncanny ability to accurately work complex mathematical procedures in his mind. In his dreams, he was visited by the Hindu goddess Namakkal, who would present him with mathematical formulae. Later, he would verify them.

LABYRINTH: A labyrinth suggests confusion. Someone will work out a problem or solve a mystery. *See also* Maze.

LACE: Lace represents extravagance and luxury.

LADDER: If someone is climbing the ladder, they can expect to reach lofty goals. If someone is climbing down the ladder, they can expect minor delays before success.

LADYBUG: Proper and polite behavior is called for. A ladybug is a sign of good luck if it is seen walking over green leaves. *See also* Bugs and Leaf.

LAKE: If calm, await a peaceful and restful time. If rough, anticipate troubled times. *See also* Water.

LAME: Progress may be slow.

LANDSLIDE: To observe a landslide from afar means obstacles have been avoided. To be caught in a landslide indicates someone is carrying too many responsibilities.

LANTERN: To dream of a lantern predicts a newfound understanding of difficulties. To put out a lantern (or light) means the dissolving of a partnership. *See also* Light.

LAP: Sitting on someone's lap foreshadows a new love affair. Seeing someone on someone else's lap portends confusion and conflicting stories. *See also* Affair.

LAPIS LAZULI: Lapis lazuli is a symbol of luxury and perfection. *See also* Gems.

LASSO: If someone uses a lasso successfully, pleasant opportunities may come their way. If someone uses it awkwardly, opportunities may be missed. *See also* Horse and Rodeo.

LAUGH: To laugh in a dream foretells happy times ahead. To hear laughter is a warning to avoid creating an embarrassing situation.

LAUNDRY: If laundry is soiled, something requires attention. If it's clean, a fresh start is indicated. *See also* Hamper.

LAVA: Flowing lava is a sign of repressed emotions seeping to the surface. *See also* Volcano.

LAVENDER: Lavender is representative of enjoyable times with old friends, perhaps at a family or high school reunion. *See also* Flowers.

LAWYER: Someone may need professional help in business or legal matters. *See also* Courthouse, Judge, and Jury.

LEAF: Green leaves predict abundance and prosperity. Falling leaves denote the end of relationships. *See also* Ladybug, Rake, Trees, and individual plant listings.

LEAK: Someone is wasting their efforts. They should channel their energies in a more positive direction. *See also* Plumbing and Water.

LEASH: A leash represents restrictions and limits. *See also* individual animal listings.

LECTURE: Do you feel like you are being talked down to? Are you talking down to someone else? Listen to opinions.

LEECH: Someone depends on you too much for support and is draining you emotionally. Set boundaries.

LEGS: Legs are means of support. They indicate a solid foundation. *See also* Knee.

LEMON: A lemon portends social embarrassments. *See also* Food.

LETTER: A letter is a means of communication. Someone will receive news from far away. *See also* Ink, Paper, Parcel, Post Office, and Writing.

LEVITATE: To observe someone levitating represents a change in mood, or a lessening of depression. To levitate in a dream indicates that someone may rise above a situation and become more objective in their opinions.

LIBRARY: A library signifies knowledge and information. *See also* Book and Page.

LICENSE: A license is a symbol of permission and freedom. Someone is able to proceed with plans and may experience little interference or setbacks.

LICK: To lick something means someone's pride has been hurt, but they will soon lick their own wounds.

LIFEGUARD: A lifeguard is a symbol of the inner wisdom that guides one's life. *See also* Swim.

LIGHT: Light indicates spiritual energy and guidance. If a light comes on, someone may be enlightened or something may be made clear to them. *See also* Lantern, Lighthouse, Searchlight, and Shadow.

LIGHTHOUSE: A lighthouse is a sign of guidance and assistance through troubled times. It is a beacon, a port in the storm. *See also* Light and Searchlight.

LIGHTNING: Luck will strike—out of the blue! *See also* Cloud, Rain, Sky, Storm, and Thunder.

LILAC: Look for pleasant days ahead. *See also* Flowers.

LIMOUSINE: Seeing a limousine drive by is a sign of missed opportunities. Riding in a limousine indicates that someone may be offered the opportunity to develop their talents and ideas. *See also* Car.

LION: A lion is representative of a brave and strong person, one who can be relied on for support.

LIVING ROOM: Someone is enjoying being the center of attention.

LIZARD: First appearances may indicate an unfavorable character, but look more closely to see that this is not the case.

LOBSTER: Embarrassments will soon be forgotten.

LOCK: A lock presents an obstacle. If a key is in the dream or there is a way to open the lock, the obstacle will be overcome. *See also* Key.

LOFT: Someone has lofty goals that may be hard to achieve.

LOST: Being lost implies feelings of insecurity. If someone else is lost, it indicates that you should contact that person. *See also* Map.

LOTTERY: Winning the lottery foretells of a lucky break. Someone may hear good news. *See also* Money and Wealth.

LOTUS: The archetype is represented by the higher or inner self, perfection, and purity. *See also* Flowers and Yoga.

LUGGAGE: Luggage in dreams forecasts personal and emotional baggage. Do you carry it with you? If the luggage is present in unusual circumstances, you should deal with something and let it go. *See also* Journey, Pilgrimage, and Quest.

MAGIC: Magic symbolizes unexpected changes. *See also* Magician and Wand.

MAGICIAN: The archetype is represented by the keeper of wisdom and knowledge. *See also* Magic and Wand.

MAGNET: A magnet implies sexual attractiveness and flirtation.

MAGNIFYING GLASS: A magnifying glass portends an increase in finances.

MALE: The archetype is represented by masculine qualities, strength, the provider, and the intellect.

MANSION: A mansion is an image of the inner or spiritual self. *See also* House.

MAP: Someone will point you in the right direction. *See also* Atlas and Lost.

MAPLE TREE: A maple tree symbolizes prosperity and growth due to diversity and cooperation. *See also* Leaf and Trees.

MARBLE: A marble represents the past. Someone is dwelling upon past events.

MARKET: Decisions and choices must be made shortly.

MARRIAGE: The archetype is represented by a merging of masculine and feminine energies. *See also* Bride and Bridegroom.

MARS: To dream of the planet indicates conflicts, misunderstandings, or arguments of a petty nature. *See also* Alien and Planets.

MARSH: Does someone feel bogged down? Who is it? Why? Progress will be slow, but goals will be achieved. *See also* Swamp.

MARTYR: A martyr signifies self-sacrifice within a relationship or to ideals.

MASK: Don't be deceived by appearances. There is more to a situation or person than is obviously evident. What is behind the mask? *See also* Disguise.

MAZE: Don't know where to turn? *See also* Labyrinth.

MECHANIC: A mechanic represents someone who makes amends or apologizes for bad behavior. *See also* Car.

MEDAL: A medal is a sign that hard work has not gone unnoticed. If someone else has a medal, you may be envious of their accomplishments. *See also* Bronze, Gold, Silver, and Trophy.

MEDICINE: Medicine is a sign of healing energies, of old wounds that are healing. *See also* Ambulance, Bandage, Doctor, Needle, Nurse, Ointment, Pill, Plague, Quarantine, Rash, Surgery, Vaccination, and X Ray.

MERCURY: If the planet or in a thermometer, expect a raise either in financial matters or in social standing. *See also* Alien and Planets.

MERMAID: A mermaid denotes an exciting, fleeting romance. *See also* Merman and Water.

MERMAN: A male may capture the heart of someone, but it may be a brief affair. *See also* Mermaid and Water.

METEOR: A meteor is a warning: avoidable troubles ahead. *See also* Sky.

MICROSCOPE: A microscope indicates overreactions to small problems, making them appear bigger than they are.

MILDEW: Mildew represents unfortunate circumstances in love or friendship.

MILK: Don't cry over spilled milk. Milk is a good sign of nurturing and caring. *See also* Cow, Cream, and Thirst.

MINE: Either someone will gain wealth through their own efforts, but it will take some time, or it is a play on the word "mine" meaning ownership.

MIRROR: A mirror reflects how you see yourself or how others see you. Is the image a true likeness of who you are? Or is there distortion, a different face for the public?

MISTLETOE: Mistletoe suggests a new relationship.

MONEY: Money suggests financial matters. To find or win money is a lucky sign: Something important is coming your way. Losing money indicates a loss of emotional support. *See also* Bank, Beggar, Coins, Gold, Jackpot, Penny, Reward, Wallet, and Wealth.

MONKEY: Beware of monkey business, mischief, and deceit! A monkey in a zoo implies troubles in the workplace. A monkey in the jungle is a sign of trouble in a relationship.

MONSTER: The archetype is represented by an expression of inner fears.

MOON: Several meanings are associated with the moon, depending on its appearance. In general, the moon is a sign of good luck. A new moon suggests success with new projects; a full moon indicates success in affairs of the heart; and a harvest moon implies financial rewards. *See also* Alien, Eclipse, and Planets.

MOONSTONE: It is a symbol of mystical forces and spiritual experiences. *See also* Gems.

Alexander's Great Dreams

When Alexander the Great campaigned throughout the Persian Empire, he employed soothsayer Aristander of Telmessos, who had written a book on dreams, as his personal dream interpreter.

MOP: A clean mop is a sign that an enjoyable activity, like a hobby, could become profitable. A dirty mop suggests neglected responsibilities. *See also* Broom, Dust, Housekeeper, and Sweep.

MOSQUITO: A mosquito is a pest. Set boundaries when people place unreasonable demands. *See also* Bugs.

MOSS: Green, healthy moss predicts romantic excitement. Old, dry moss indicates disappointment and doubt. *See also* Woods.

MOTHER: The archetype is represented by a feminine authority figure, the nurturer, and fertility.

MOUNTAIN: A mountain symbolizes high standards. If someone is climbing a mountain, they will rise in power and authority in their work. If someone is descending, they will suffer setbacks. *See also* Hill.

MOUSE: Keep to yourself for a while before voicing opinions.

MOUTH: An open mouth with teeth showing warns of a false friend. An open mouth with no teeth showing suggests opinions should not be given. A closed mouth indicates a new friendship. *See also* Dentist, Spit, Tongue, and Tooth.

MUSEUM: Old friends and memories are important now.

MUSIC: It means harmony and peace of mind if the music is pleasant. If discordant or noisy, it foreshadows a lack of harmony in a relationship. *See also* Bagpipes, Carol, Drum, Fiddle, Horn, Humming, Orchestra, Piano, Quartet, Radio, Sing, Trumpet, Violin, Xylophone, and Yodel.

MUSK: The smell of musk portends a new, exciting, passionate love affair. *See also* Odor and Perfume.

MUTE: To be mute indicates that you may be too withdrawn. To see a mute person implies someone may not be voicing their opinions enough.

NAG: Someone might want to get things off their chest by confiding in a close friend.

NAIL: Someone will succeed through their own hard work and effort. *See also* Hammer.

NAKED: Nakedness is exposure. All will be revealed.

NAP: Take time out from a problem. A solution will come when you are less involved.

NAPKIN: A folded napkin is a sign of happy social activities in the near future. *See also* Food, Fork, Plate, and Spoon.

NAVEL: If your own, a symbol of good luck with long-range plans. If someone else's, a new love may soon be yours.

NECK: Money is coming very shortly. If the neck is broken, it implies poor money management; pay closer attention to your budget. *See also* Necklace, Necktie, and Scarf.

NECKLACE: A necklace is a good omen for a love relationship. However, if broken, it forewarns of domestic conflict. *See also* Gems and Neck.

NECKTIE: A necktie implies a relationship should be ended. *See also* Neck.

NEEDLE: Is something needling you? If a sewing needle, something needs mending in your immediate circumstances. If an inoculation, it is protection against illness. *See also* Knit, Medicine, Sewing, Thimble, Thread, and Vaccination.

NEST: A nest is a represen-tation of the home. If full of eggs, await financial gain (as in a nest egg). *See also* Birds, Eggs, and individual bird listings.

NET: Expect entanglements and traps ahead. Be alert! *See also* Fish.

NIGHTINGALE: Romance may soon find its way to you. *See also* Birds.

NOSE: Someone is being nosy! Guard secrets if they shouldn't be revealed.

NUGGET: To receive a nugget of gold predicts an opportunity that promises to develop into something bigger and better than originally hoped for. *See also* Gold and Pan.

NUN: A nun either means denial and self-sacrifice, or indicates a habit or repetitive action that should be curbed. *See also* Abbey, Altar, Church, Convent, and Priest.

NURSE: A nurse signifies the need for assistance in some-one's life. *See also* Medicine.

NUT: A nut predicts great potential for future endeav-ors. *See also* Peanut and Walnut.

OAK: An oak indicates a strong marriage and family life. If many acorns are around the oak, there will be many children. *See also* Acorn, Leaf, and Woods.

OAR: Someone will triumph because of their own willpower. If rowing smoothly with two oars, they will succeed with ease. If they have only one oar, they may go in circles for a while; it may be wise to get help. *See also* Canoe, Raft, and Water.

OASIS: An oasis is an omen of success and profit when least expected.

OATH: To take an oath means that a serious commitment will be made that must be seen through to the end.

OATS: Oats are good omens for business dealings. *See also* Fields, Horse, and Pasture.

OCEAN: An ocean is a reflection of emotions. If calm, emotions are peaceful. If stormy, there are turbulent ups and downs and emotional conflicts. *See also* Beach, Seashells, Ship, Spray, Submarine, Tidal Wave, Tide, Water, and individual animal listings.

OCTOPUS: Someone has many challenges but will get through them with ease.

ODOR: If pleasant, it is a good sign. If unpleasant, it is a warning of problems. *See also* Incense, Musk, and Perfume.

OFFICE: Someone is working on self-improvement.

OFFICER: An officer is an authority figure demanding respect and obedience, and a sign of security and protection. *See also* Uniform.

OIL: To dream of striking oil is a prediction of riches and good fortune. To oil machinery is a sign that things are working well.

OINTMENT: Ointment represents a healing balm. It can soothe emotional turmoil. *See also* Medicine.

OLIVES: Olives represent happiness and contentment. *See also* Food and Olive Tree.

OLIVE TREE: An olive tree indicates peace and serenity. *See also* Food, Leaf, Olive, and Trees.

ONION: Tears may be shed, but they are not sincere. Someone is wearing a false face to gain sympathy. *See also* Food.

ONYX: Someone may be living beyond their means. They might want to cut back on spending. *See also* Gems.

OPAL: An opal predicts unexpected good fortune. *See also* Gems.

ORANGE: The color orange is a symbol of the emotions, creativity, and new beginnings. The fruit indicates happiness and sunny days ahead. *See also* Food.

ORCHARD: An orchard foreshadows good luck and prosperity. Projects will flourish. *See also* individual fruit listings.

ORCHESTRA: Are you in tune with others? Check facts before giving opinions. *See also* Music and individual instrument listings.

ORCHIDS: Orchids suggest forbidden, passionate love. *See also* Flowers.

OSTRICH: Don't bury your head in the sand. Be more aware of what is going on around you. *See also* Birds.

OVEN: An event may soon change someone's life for the better. *See also* Cooking, Food, Kitchen, Stove, and individual food listings.

OVERALLS: Overalls represent someone with a calm, down-to-earth nature.

PADDLE WHEEL: Things seem to be progressing slowly, but in fact much is being accomplished at this time. *See also* Water.

PAGE: Turning pages in a book symbolizes turning over a leaf and starting anew. A blank page implies a fresh, clean start. *See also* Book, Diary, Ink, Library, Paper, and Writing.

PAIL: If full, a sign of abundance. If empty, a sign something is lacking. It may also be a word soundalike for *pale*, indicating illness or weakness.

PAINT: If the paint is new, it implies restoration. If it is flaking or peeling, it suggests a business idea is not as sound as it appears. *See also* Enamel, Painting, and Palette.

PAINTING: If a picture, it indicates an unrealistic view. If someone is in the act of painting, watch that something important is not being covered up or hidden. *See also* Paint and Palette.

PALACE: A palace is a good omen for financial gain, luxury, and leisure. *See also* Castle, Joker, King, Knight, Prince, Princess, and Queen.

PALETTE: A palette indicates many talents and successful pursuits. *See also* Paint and Painting.

PALLBEARER: A pallbearer is a good sign that old burdens are now laid to rest. *See also* Cemetery and Death.

PALM TREE: Tropical symbolism implies vacations and romantic getaways. *See also* Leaf and Trees.

PAN: If panning for gold, something is sought that may be difficult to achieve. *See also* Gold and Nugget.

PANCAKES: Eating pancakes implies boredom with family matters. *See also* Food.

PANIC: Panic suggests someone has jumped to a wrong conclusion.

PANSY: Enjoy the simple things. *See also* Flowers.

PANTHER: A panther is a sign of an intelligent thinker with an agile mind.

PANTRY: Someone is well organized and never at a loss for ideas. *See also* Food.

PANTS: Who wears the pants? Someone is neglecting their responsibilities.

PANTYHOSE: Things are not as they seem. Don't judge something by appearance only. *See also* Tights.

PAPER: There is a desire to write. *See also* Book, Diary, Ink, Letter, Page, Parchment, Quill, and Writing.

PARACHUTE: If descending by means of a parachute, the parachute symbolizes safety

and a favorable outcome. *See also* Airplane.

PARADE: If watching a parade, does someone feel like life is passing by? If in a parade, someone will soon be celebrating a promotion or bonus. *See also* Clown.

PARADISE: Things are too good to be true. Examine the details.

PARCEL: To dream of receiving a parcel in the mail can be a literal interpretation: Soon a package via post will come. To send a parcel implies something is being given from one person to another. *See also* Letter and Post Office.

PARCHMENT: A valuable document may be placed in your or someone else's care. Be sure to read the fine print. *See also* Paper.

PARK: To go to a park suggests easy times ahead. To

park a car implies a pause or standstill with a work-related project. *See also* Car.

PAROLE: Parole means something is being restricted. *See also* Police.

PARROT: Don't repeat idle gossip. *See also* Birds.

PASSENGER: You are "being taken for a ride." Question a friend's intentions. *See also* Car and U Turn.

PASSPORT: A passport signifies freedom to explore different aspects of life. This is a good time for personal development. *See also* Journey, Luggage, Pilgrimage, and Quest.

PASTURE: Is it time to put something out to pasture, like old habits or worn-out ideas? *See also* Fields, Grain, Oats, Plow, and individual animal listings.

A Father and Son Guided by Dreams

Italian poet Dante Alighieri claimed that his work, *The Divine Comedy,* was told to him in a dream on Good Friday in 1300. After his death in 1321, part of the manuscript could not be found, so it was assumed that it was unfinished. His son Jacob, however, didn't believe the manuscript was unfinished, but he was unable to find it anywhere. Jacob dreamed that Dante came to him and answered many of his questions concerning the afterlife. When asked about the remainder of the manuscript, Dante led Jacob to a room that he had often slept in when alive. He touched the wall and said, "What you have sought for so much is here," and then he disappeared. When Jacob woke, he found the missing pages where his dream had indicated.

PATCH: To dream of patching something implies forgiveness of others. *See also* Needle, Sewing, Thimble, and Thread.

PATH: This implies the path through life. Is the path smooth and free of obstacles, or are there some twists and turns ahead? *See also* Crossroads and Fork.

PATIO: Some family concerns should be kept private. Be discreet when talking with neighbors. *See also* House.

PATTERN: If an intricate pattern, there's a lot on someone's mind but that person is well organized. If a simple pattern, there's a routine schedule in life.

PAVEMENT: The path ahead is clear and easy to travel. *See also* Pothole.

PAW: If an animal extends its paw, it is a sign that an acquaintance may be made soon who will become a close friend. *See also* individual animal listings.

PAWNBROKER: If you dream of selling to a pawnbroker, you may be selling yourself short and you may not give yourself enough credit for your achievements. It's not true. Give yourself a pat on the back!

PEA: A pea means ideas are not insignificant like they are thought to be. Voice opinions at the workplace. *See also* Food.

PEACH: Someone will be made an offer they can't refuse. *See also* Food.

PEACOCK: It's time to get out there and strut your stuff! *See also* Birds.

PEANUT: Is someone getting paid what they are worth, or are they working for peanuts? *See also* Food and Nut.

PEARL: A pearl is an omen of good health. *See also* Gems.

PEDESTAL: Is someone on a pedestal? Try to see authority figures in a more realistic light.

PELICANS: Pelicans predict an invitation to a festive and casual event, like a beach party or barbecue. Enjoy! *See also* Birds.

PENGUIN: Does someone feel like just another face in the crowd? It's time to express individuality. *See also* Birds.

PENNY: A penny for your thoughts? Someone is intrigued by you and wants to get to know you. *See also* Bank, Coins, and Money.

PENSION: News will be received of a substantial windfall within your family.

PENTHOUSE: A penthouse indicates someone has high standards not many people can live up to. *See also* House.

PEPPER: Time to spice up your life. Have fun with friends! *See also* Food and Salt.

PEPPERMINTS: Someone has more energy lately and feels like tackling all those little odd jobs around the house. *See also* Food.

PERCOLATOR: A percolator indicates ideas concerning new business ventures; wait for better conditions before taking action. *See also* Thirst.

PERFUME: To smell perfume in a dream is a sign of good luck. *See also* Musk and Odor.

PERISCOPE: Someone has a great ability to see beyond the obvious. *See also* Ship and Submarine.

PERSPIRATION: Someone has been working hard. Take a break!

PETAL: Love and romance are soon going to overwhelm thoughts. *See also* Blossom,

Bud, Flowers, and individual flower listings.

PEWTER: An object made of pewter is a sign of financial comfort.

PHOTOGRAPH: Memories of the past occupy thoughts. Catch up with an old friend.

PIANO: To dream of hearing a piano predicts a favorable surprise. *See also* Music.

PICKET: To dream of people picketing means you strongly disagree with something or someone, and it is demanding too much of your attention. A picket fence implies that there are unrealistic ideas in a relationship. *See also* Fence and Gate.

PICKLE: Is someone in a pickle? Is there a situation that is difficult to get out of? Why? *See also* Food.

PICKPOCKET: A pickpocket suggests someone feels taken for granted or overlooked in the workplace. *See also* Thief.

PICNIC: A picnic is a good omen of a comfortable family life. *See also* Blanket and Food.

PIG: A pig indicates a lazy, careless person.

PIGEON: A pigeon predicts someone may receive word from a long-lost friend. *See also* Birds.

PIGGYBACK: If you are carrying someone, you have taken on another's problems. If you are being carried, you are relying too much on someone else's advice.

PILGRIMAGE: A pilgrimage is an indication of a spiritual journey of self-discovery. *See also* Journey, Luggage, Passport, Pioneer, and Quest.

PILL: Is something hard to swallow? There's more to a story than meets the eye. *See also* Medicine.

PILLARS: Pillars are symbols of support and strength.

PILLOW: Don't overlook the obvious; more rest may be necessary at this time. *See also* Bed, Bedroom, Blanket, and Quilt.

PILOT: Someone may be helped through a difficult time by one who has experienced a similar situation. *See also* Airplane and Helicopter.

PIMPLE: A pimple is an omen of an embarrassing situation that will soon be forgotten.

PINE: Are you pining over someone? Pine trees suggest time is needed to think about a situation carefully before making decisions. *See also* Leaf, Pinecone, and Trees.

PINEAPPLE: A prickly predicament will turn out in someone's favor. *See also* Food.

PINECONE: Something seemingly unimportant will prove advantageous. *See also* Pine.

PINK: Someone is "tickled pink" and may enjoy happiness and affection.

PIONEER: Forge ahead with plans. Your plans will bring success and recognition of ingenuity. *See also* Journey, Pilgrimage, and Quest.

PIRATE: Someone refuses to play by the rules. This kind of behavior can result in unfavorable circumstances. *See also* Plank, Ship, and Treasure.

PITCH: This is a good time to present or discuss ideas with a boss. *See also* Ball, Bat, and Pitcher.

PITCHER: If a baseball pitcher, be wary of spoken words. If a water pitcher, there is unused potential at your fingertips; you can achieve goals. *See also* Ball, Bat, Pitch, and Water.

PITCHFORK: Making hay? A pitchfork is a sign of a passionate love affair not too far into the future.

PLAGUE: Something is troublesome and, if not dealt with, could get out of hand. *See also* Medicine.

PLAID: Expect happy and festive times ahead.

PLANETS: Someone has lofty goals that could come true. The sky is the limit! *See also* Alien, Mars, Mercury, Moon, Sky, Star, and Universe.

PLANK: Do you feel like you're walking the plank, as if there is little choice in present circumstances? Don't despair—there is a way out. *See also* Pirate and Ship.

PLAQUE: Someone will be recognized for achievements in a surprising way.

PLASTER: Something concealed will soon be revealed.

PLASTIC: Something or someone is a phony, an imitation of the real thing.

PLATE: If full, does someone have too much on their plate? *See also* Food, Fork, Napkin, and Spoon.

PLATFORM: A platform is a symbol of a rise in career or status.

PLAYGROUND: Get in touch with the inner child, and have some fun!

PLOW: With patience and determination, plowing through obstacles currently in the path will be made possible. *See also* Fields and Pasture.

PLUM: A plum points to the ideal choice. To dream of eating plums indicates making the right decision about something is important. *See also* Food.

PLUMBER: A plumber represents one who is efficient and keeps things running smoothly. *See also* Plumbing.

PLUMBING: Life will hold some twists and turns over the next few weeks, but all will be fine in the end. *See also* Leak.

POCKET: A pocket indicates financial abundance and security.

POEM: A poem implies a dedication, a sign of respect and honor. If a romantic poem, there may be a secret admirer. *See also* Writing.

POISON: Avoid a heated argument if possible. Words will be spoken that cannot be taken back.

POLICE: Dreaming of police is a sign of security and protection. *See also* Parole.

POLKA DOTS: Someone needs more variety in life. A change of scene or a new hobby would improve the quality of life.

POND: A pond signifies calmness and peace of mind. *See also* Water.

POOL: Perhaps you and an associate should pool resources? Pools also symbolize hope and promise. *See also* Swim and Water.

POPCORN: Popcorn foretells much activity. *See also* Food.

POPLAR TREE: Someone may enjoy popularity at a social function. *See also* Leaf and Trees.

POPPY: Remembrance of past hardships puts perspective on current difficulties. *See also* Flowers.

PORCH: Someone may be offered more responsibility in the workplace as a result of a job well done. *See also* House.

Waking Up Inside a Dream

Sometimes you can realize you are dreaming while you are still dreaming. This is called *lucid dreaming* and can happen involuntarily. Dr. Stephen LaBerge, founder of the Lucidity Institute, demonstrated that, with practice and determination, anyone can learn to have lucid dreams. Once you are lucid in your dream, you can control much of your dream environment and enjoy such feats as flying, walking through walls, and changing scenes.

PORCUPINE: Handle a prickly situation with care!

PORTHOLE: A perspective of an issue should be broadened; the whole picture is not being seen. *See also* Ship and Submarine.

POST OFFICE: Communications and negotiations are slow, but important news may soon arrive. *See also* Letter and Parcel.

POTATO: A potato is a representation of the basic essentials in life. *See also* Food.

POTHOLE: A rough road is ahead, but it will soon smooth out. *See also* Pavement.

POTTERY: Pottery suggests domestic happiness. Broken pottery warns of broken promises. *See also* Sculpt.

POWDER: Beware of false appearances.

PRAIRIE: Prairie lands imply great potential for abundance in monetary matters.

PRANK: To dream of playing a prank means someone is not taking something seriously enough. To have a prank played is a reminder to not take things so seriously.

PREACHER: Does someone practice what they preach? Make sure conversation is not one-sided. Be sure to listen. *See also* Altar and Church.

PREGNANT: Pregnancy is a good omen that a new project or endeavor is coming after a period of incubation. *See also* Baby and Birth.

PRESERVES: Making preserves symbolizes happy childhood memories. *See also* Jam and individual fruit listings.

PRIEST: The archetype is represented by the part of personality concerned with spiritual matters. *See also* Abbey, Altar, Church, and Nun.

PRINCE: A male will enter someone's life soon and will become very important to that person. *See also* Castle, Crown, Palace, and Throne.

PRINCESS: Expect to be treated like royalty very soon!

See also Castle, Palace, Throne, and Tiara.

PRODIGY: To dream of a prodigy, or genius, suggests that hidden talents may soon be drawn upon.

PROJECT: Working on a project represents someone's goals and aspirations. If the work is progressing easily, the goals may be attained with ease. If the work appears to be haphazard, it is a sign that someone's goals are not clearly defined.

PROPOSAL: An important decision must be made. Don't choose in haste.

PUDDLE: Take care of the small things in life, and the big things will take care of themselves. *See also* Rain.

PULLEY: With little effort, a lot of work can be accomplished. Things are running smoothly and efficiently.

PUMPKIN: A pumpkin signals financial gain in a series of small successes, possibly several sales. *See also* Food.

PUPPET: Someone behind the scenes is pulling the strings.

PURPLE: The color purple symbolizes luxury, royalty, lawfulness, and order.

PUZZLE: Things come in bits and pieces, but eventually all will fall into place.

QUAIL: To dream of this bird symbolizes a lack of self-esteem. *See also* Birds.

QUARANTINE: To dream someone is put into quarantine suggests a need to withdraw attention from a preoccupation. Spend more time in self-reflection. *See also* Medicine.

QUARREL: There are two sides to an issue. Be sure to be well informed of both. *See also* Duel.

QUARTET: A musical quartet signifies domestic harmony. *See also* Music and individual instrument listings.

QUARTZ: If clear, it is an omen of monetary gain. If smoky, it signifies indecision. If pink, it is a sign of success. *See also* Gems.

QUEEN: The archetype is represented by equality, emotions, harmony, and intuitive guidance. *See also* Castle, Palace, Throne, and Tiara.

QUEST: Inner or spiritual growth is important as meaning and purpose are sought. *See also* Journey, Luggage, Passport, Pilgrimage, and Pioneer.

QUESTIONNAIRE: What do you really want? Be clear about what you want as opposed to what you think you want.

QUICKSAND: Don't get stuck in a situation that may be difficult to get out of; don't make promises that can't be kept.

QUIET: If everything is quiet in a dream, expect a period of peacefulness over the next few days.

QUILL: A sharp-tongued comment could cause problems. Don't share opinions with others. *See also* Ink, Paper, and Writing.

QUILT: A quilt is a good omen of financial security in old age. *See also* Bed, Bedroom, Blanket, and Pillow.

QUIVER: If someone or something is quivering in a dream, it implies emotional disturbances over trivial matters.

QUIZ: If taking a quiz, potential or worth is being assessed by an authority figure, perhaps an employer.

QUOTATION: To hear or repeat a quote indicates little self-confidence in opinions. (Be sure to identify and interpret the quotation as well.)

RABBIT: A rabbit is a sign of fertility, abundance, and productivity.

RACKET (SPORTS): Don't get involved in unappealing activities. They could be more than anticipated. *See also* Table Tennis and Tennis.

RADIATION: Either you or an acquaintance is giving off vibes of a romantic nature, and someone else is taking notice! *See also* X Ray.

RADIO: Listen to the inner voice, and disregard outside opinions. *See also* Music.

RAFFLE: A raffle suggests a good time for spring-cleaning. Toss out anything that is no longer useful.

RAFT: A raft is a symbol of isolation and indecision, as though someone is merely drifting through their days. *See also* Oar and Water.

RAFTERS: Rafters signify someone is bothered by nagging thoughts. *See also* House.

RAID: A raid indicates vulnerability. *See also* Riot.

RAILROAD: A railroad predicts a short journey. *See also* Train.

RAIN: Rain cleanses the spirit and washes troubles away. *See also* Cloud, Hail, Lightning, Puddle, Rainbow, Sky, Storm, and Thunder.

RAINBOW: A rainbow is an indication of harmony, balance, and completion. It represents a smooth course after a time of expended effort and learned lessons. The pot of gold is waiting! *See also* Cloud, Gold, Rain, and Sky.

RAISINS: Raisins are signs of good fortune. *See also* Food and Grapes.

RAKE: Make domestic matters a priority, and take care of anything that requires attention. *See also* Leaf.

RAM: A ram points to aggressiveness and assertive behavior. *See also* Horn.

RANCH: Things appear quiet on the outside, but on the inside there is much work and activity. *See also* individual animal listings.

RASH: Minor irritations are causing disturbances in the workforce. Deal with them soon, before the problems become more complicated. *See also* Medicine.

RASPBERRY: It implies defiance from an unexpected source. *See also* Food.

RATTLE: Things need to be shaken up! Put a little variety into your routine. *See also* Baby.

RECEPTION: A wedding reception predicts success with business partnerships. *See also* Marriage.

RECIPE: Everything needed to proceed with a plan or project is available. *See also* Cooking, Food, and individual food listings.

RECYCLE: Something thought to have no value will turn out to be very useful. *See also* Garbage and Junk.

RED: The color red represents energy, physical strength, and fiery emotions.

REDWOOD TREE: A symbol of endurance, patience, and longevity. *See also* Leaf and Trees.

REEF: A hidden message may be revealed. *See also* Water.

REFEREE: Someone may bring harmony and resolution to an unsettled situation. *See also* individual sport listings.

REFRIGERATOR: It is time to proceed with something that was on hold. If someone doesn't act soon, something will not come to fruition. *See also* Food, Freezer, Kitchen, Thirst, and individual beverage and food listings.

RENT: Paying rent is a reminder that you owe someone a favor.

REPTILE: A disagreeable person will cause discomfort in a personal relationship.

RESERVOIR: A reservoir is a personal storehouse of energy. Is the reservoir full or depleted? *See also* Water.

RESTAURANT: A restaurant is a symbol of sustenance. It may also be a play on the phrase "rest or rant." Is someone going to grin and bear it, or is someone going to let it all out? *See also* Food and Waitstaff.

RETIRE: Someone retiring is a sign that something has run its course and is at an end.

REUNION: An important connection will be made between two seemingly different events.

REWARD: If a reward is offered, someone's work and abilities are being praised to others. *See also* Money.

RHINESTONE: Rhinestones suggest false friends. Someone is not being completely honest. *See also* Gems.

RHINOCEROS: If in the wild, a rhinoceros is a symbol of fertility. A rhinoceros in a cage is a sign that a trip or an event may be cancelled.

RHUBARB: Unexpected visitors may arrive shortly. *See also* Food.

RIBBON: A ribbon symbolizes kept promises.

RICE: Someone may soon hear of a hasty wedding, possibly an elopement. *See also* Food.

RIDING: If someone is riding an animal well, it foretells of success using inborn talents. If someone is riding poorly, it implies more learning and accomplishments are necessary. *See also* Horse.

RIGGING: A sailing ship's rigging indicates ideas and plans are taking shape. *See also* Captain, Sailor, and Ship.

RING: A ring is a token of love and affection. *See also* Gems.

RINK: Skating in a rink predicts easy business success. *See also* Skating.

RIOT: To see or hear of a riot foretells disagreements in the workplace. To participate in a riot is an expression of pent-up feelings. *See also* Raid.

RIVAL: If the dream is of someone who is a rival, there will soon be confrontation.

RIVER: Is someone going with the flow or fighting the current? *See also* Water.

ROAST: To roast meat predicts someone will question the integrity of a friend's word. *See also* Food.

ROBOT: Some activity has become routine and boring. It's time for a change.

ROCK: A rock signifies stability, strength, and endurance.

RODEO: There may be some ups and downs over the next few days, but someone may pull through triumphantly. *See also* Horse and Lasso.

ROLLING PIN: A rolling pin indicates smoothing out rough edges of a minor problem. *See also* Cooking, Food, and Recipe.

ROOF: To be under a roof is a sign of safety and security. To be on or repairing a roof is a sign a legal matter has been neglected. *See also* House.

ROOSTER: A rooster is a good omen for monetary matters. *See also* Chickens.

ROOT: Someone is getting to the root of the matter, or it could be a word soundalike for *route*—meaning life's direction. *See also* Garden.

ROSE: A rose indicates love and affection. Someone is thinking of you fondly. *See also* Flowers and Thorn.

ROULETTE: Don't gamble when it comes to romance.

RUBY: A ruby is a symbol of good luck, particularly in travel. *See also* Gems.

RUFFLES: Frivolous details are distracting someone from more important matters.

RUNNING: Is someone running toward or away from something? What? Why?

SADDLE: Back in the saddle again! You are ready for action! *See also* Horse.

SAILOR: Someone or something will enter someone else's life for a short time and leave a lasting impression. *See also* Captain, Rigging, and Ship.

SALT: Someone may be recognized and honored for their wisdom. *See also* Food and Pepper.

SANDPAPER: Someone is being rubbed the wrong way by an abrasive personality. Used and discarded sandpaper is an indication of minor annoyances.

SANDWICH: Feeling caught in the middle of a sticky situation? *See also* Food.

SAPPHIRE: An interesting opportunity may come to someone out of the blue. *See also* Gems.

SATELLITE: Someone will become more involved with an acquaintance.

SAW: A handsaw implies hard work with little recognition or reward. A chainsaw is an indication that old ties are being severed and new relationships are forming.

SCAFFOLD: A scaffold indicates restoration and reconstruction of old plans that had been previously put aside.

SCAR: A scar is a reminder of past hurts.

SCARECROW: Someone is trying to put you off of an idea or keep you from finding out the truth about something. *See also* Birds.

SCARF: If it is worn around the neck, someone might want to keep silent about personal matters. If it is not being worn, someone may hear some intriguing gossip. *See also* Neck.

SCHOOL: A school represents life's lessons. What is someone learning? *See also* Teacher and University.

SCIENTIST: A scientist implies someone who is very rigid in their thinking and who would be wise to exercise their intuitive side.

SCISSORS: Scissors symbolize cutting away the ties that bind. If someone is using scissors, someone is successfully ridding their life of unnecessary burdens. If scissors are unused, perhaps it's time someone decided what should be cut.

SCORE: Is someone keeping score? Maybe it's time to stop comparing.

SCORPION: Act with tact and be discreet. Avoid sharp words with colleagues. *See also* Bugs.

SCRAPBOOK: Memories of the past resurface, perhaps in the form of a class reunion. *See also* Photograph.

SCREAM: A scream is an expression of anger. It is a

good symbol of emotional release.

SCREWDRIVER: If a screwdriver is being used, it indicates someone may make important business connections.

SCULPT: To sculpt in a dream means you are the creator of your reality. If viewing sculpture, you have not yet fully realized you have choices and control over your destiny. *See also* Pottery.

SEAHORSE: This intriguing animal symbolizes unique abilities and special talents.

SEAL: A seal symbolizes either a playful, adventurous spirit or a "seal" of approval.

SEARCHLIGHT: Someone will be guided by close friends and colleagues in their search for purpose and meaning. *See also* Light and Lighthouse.

SEASHELLS: Expect to hear kind words from a respected authority. *See also* Beach and Ocean.

SEATBELT: Someone is acting with restraint and patience where a personal conflict is concerned. *See also* Car.

SEEDS: Seeds represent ideas that will develop into successful endeavors. *See also* Flowers and Garden.

SEWING: If someone is sewing, a relationship that had been strained will be reconciled. *See also* Knit, Needle, Patch, Thimble, and Thread.

SHADOW: The archetype is represented by the part of personality that isn't for show. A shadow symbolizes intimate thoughts. *See also* Light.

SHEEP: Is someone just going along with the crowd?

Remember to be true. *See also* Ranch.

SHELF: It's time to stop procrastinating and get those little odd jobs taken care of.

SHIP: A ship is an indication of smooth sailing—full steam ahead! *See also* Anchor, Captain, Harbor, Ocean, Periscope, Pirate, Plank, Porthole, Rigging, Sailor, Submarine, Torpedo, Water, and Yacht.

SHIRT: Emotions are guarded where affairs of the heart are concerned.

SHOES: Shoes signify steps taken to reach goals. Are you wearing your shoes or someone else's? Do you feel you should follow someone else's methods or strike out on your own? *See also* Boots, Feet, and Footprints.

SHOP: If someone is shopping, it suggests a search for solutions to relationship problems. *See also* Stores.

SHORTS: Plans for a trip may be unexpectedly cut short.

SHOULDERS: Shoulders are signs of strength, reliability, and support.

SHOVEL: Someone is not quite telling the truth, but it is a harmless exaggeration.

SHOWER: To take a shower is a sign of a release of some daily responsibilities. *See also* Bathroom, Towel, and Water.

SIGNATURE: To sign papers represents an important commitment. *See also* Writing.

SILO: A silo implies a storehouse of knowledge. It indicates that someone is a deep thinker with many ideas, but they have yet to put the ideas to use. *See also* Grain.

SILVER: Sometimes second best is the best choice. Don't

overlook all options. *See also* Medal.

SING: To hear singing in a dream is a sign troubled times are over. *See also* Carol, Music, Quartet, and Yodel.

SISTER: The archetype is represented by the emotions.

SKATING: If someone is skating well, they will accomplish their goal easily in a short time period. *See also* Rink.

SKELETON: A skeleton means revealed secrets. If you have been dishonest, someone can see right through you. *See also* Bones and Fossil.

SKULL: A skull suggests a discovery that may bring profit in business. *See also* Bones and Skeleton.

SKUNK: Something stinks! Suspicions are proved correct.

SKY: The sky is the limit! There are many opportunities available at present. *See also* Cloud, Eclipse, Hail, Lightning, Meteor, Planets, Rain, Rainbow, Star, and Storm.

SMOKE: Smoke is a warning of trouble ahead. *See also* Ashes, Burn, Fire, Firecrackers, Fireplace, and Fireworks.

SNAIL: Is someone moving at a snail's pace? Things will soon pick up.

SNAKE: A snake represents creative energy, enlightenment, and spiritual growth. If shedding its skin, it is a good omen of new beginnings and life changes.

SNOW: Snow suggests purity and wholesomeness. *See also* Arctic, Ice, Iceberg, and Icicles.

SOLITAIRE: Playing solitaire represents feelings of loneliness. *See also* Ace and Cards.

SPIDER: An ambitious and resourceful person will have

great influence in your life. *See also* Cobweb.

SPINE: The spine is a symbol representing support, responsibility, and courage. Someone may feel able to face a difficult situation. *See also* Back and Chiropractor.

SPIT: Something has left a bitter taste. The results are not satisfactory. *See also* Mouth.

SPLINTER: A splinter is indicative of nagging doubts.

SPONGE: Someone is too dependent on you, and as a result, you are feeling drained.

SPOON: Things come to someone easily. *See also* Food, Fork, Napkin, and Plate.

SPRAY: To be splashed by a spray of water is to receive blessings and good wishes on a forthcoming project. *See also* Ocean and Water.

SPRUCE TREE: Time to spruce things up and clean out unwanted clutter. *See also* Leaf and Trees.

SQUARE: A square is a symbol of balance and justice.

SQUASH: Someone may try to stop a project or cancel plans for selfish reasons. *See also* Food.

SQUIRREL: This would be a good time to plan ahead and save for a rainy day.

STAGE: Someone is at an important stage in their life. Is the stage busy with actors, indicating activity and prosperity? Or is it empty, implying rest and reflection? *See also* Audience and Theater.

STAIRS: Climbing stairs predicts a rise in status. Descending stairs suggests a lack of self-confidence.

Quit Smoking in Your Sleep

Clinical psychologist Gayle Delaney reports in her book, *All About Dreams*, that over the years several of her clients have successfully incubated dreams to help them quit smoking. Some of her clients were able to quit within a few weeks, while others were able to quit the very day after their incubated dream!

STAR: A star is a sign of good luck. Someone will achieve goals or get their wish. It can also indicate guidance, enlightenment, and insight as someone forges ahead with a meaningful project or spiritual journey. *See also* Planets, Sky, and Universe.

STARFISH: Someone adapts to new situations quickly.

STATIC: Static indicates unclear communications. *See also* Electricity.

STATUE: A statue represents an emotionless, unfeeling person.

STEW: Anger and resentment could get out of hand if not dealt with. *See also* Food.

STILTS: Stilts are representative of pride and arrogance. Are you looking down upon someone, or is someone looking down upon you?

STORES: To dream of stores means someone has everything they need at their fingertips. *See also* Shop.

STORK: A new arrival of some kind is to be expected. *See also* Birds.

STORM: A storm is an expression of rage and dissatisfaction. *See also* Cloud, Hurricane, Lightning, Rain, Sky, Thunder, and Tornado.

STOVE: Is something simmering on the back burner? Bring forward new ideas. *See also* Cooking, Food, Kitchen, Oven, and individual food listings.

STRANGER: Someone may be seen in a different light, or another side of someone's personality may be revealed.

STRAWBERRY: Expect an improvement in financial matters. *See also* Food.

STRING BEANS: There may be a short period of time during which someone may be strapped for cash. *See also* Beans and Food.

STRIPES: Someone is reluctant to change a habit or routine and, as a result, has become stuck in a rut.

STUMBLE: Someone has encountered difficulties in their path; these obstacles won't stop or deter them.

STUTTER: A stutter predicts misunderstandings due to a lack of communication.

SUBMARINE: To dream of a submarine marks explorations of the inner psyche, the subconscious. *See also* Ocean, Periscope, Porthole, Ship, Torpedo, and Water.

SUGAR: Someone has been overindulgent and too accommodating to another person. It is time to set some boundaries. *See also* Food.

SUIT: To wear a suit in a dream is a good sign that things are as they should be. To see a suit indicates something may happen only at the appropriate time.

SUN: The sun is a symbol of warmth and nurturing. Someone who has been upset or hurt may be comforted.

SUNFLOWER: An old friend may reenter your life. *See also* Flowers.

SURGERY: Surgery is a healing symbol. Someone is working on self-improvement. *See also* Medicine.

SWAMP: Does someone feel swamped? A swamp is a representation of feeling overwhelmed. *See also* Marsh.

SWAN: A swan is a symbol of beauty and grace. *See also* Birds.

SWEEP: Make a clean sweep. This is a time of resolutions in both personal and business affairs. *See also* Broom, Dust, Housekeeper, and Mop.

SWIM: If someone is swimming with their head above water, they will enjoy success. If swimming underwater, they will experience setbacks but will eventually achieve their desired results. *See also* Drowning, Lifeguard, Pool, Underwater, and Water.

SWIMSUIT: To wear a swimsuit signifies self-confidence. To see a swimsuit on a mannequin or on a sale rack implies someone lacks self-assurance. *See also* Swim.

SWORD: A sword points to strength and endurance during times of stress.

TABLE: Someone may negotiate a contract and enjoy favorable results. *See also* Chair.

TABLE TENNIS: A disagreement is going nowhere. Drop it and walk away. *See also* Ball and Racket.

TAMBOURINE: Someone may hear unfounded rumors and might want to ignore the gossip. *See also* Music.

TANGO: It takes two to tango. Don't place all the blame on just one person. *See also* Dance.

TANTRUM: Throwing a tantrum implies impatience. A child throwing a tantrum warns of childish behavior in a personal relationship.

TARGET: Goals are right on target. Go forward with plans. *See also* Arrow.

TATTOO: A seemingly permanent situation can be changed, but it will take work and ingenuity.

TEA: Sipping tea foretells pleasant days with old friends. *See also* Kettle, Thirst, and Water.

TEACHER: A teacher represents one who leads someone else along a life path. *See also* School and University.

TEAR: If someone is shedding tears, sadness will pass quickly and be followed by joy.

TELEVISION: Someone is putting more effort and energy into the affairs of others and might want to step back and take some quiet time. *See also* Cartoon and Celebrity.

TEMPLE: A temple represents the inner self or soul. *See also* Church.

TENNIS: If undecided about something, wait before making any decisions. *See also* Ball and Racket.

TENT: Find a temporary solution before a more favorable situation can be arranged. *See also* Camp.

THEATER: A theater signifies life experiences. *See also* Audience and Stage.

THIEF: A thief in a dream suggests vulnerability. *See also* Pickpocket.

THIMBLE: Someone will receive needed assistance with small details. *See also* Needle, Patch, Sewing, and Thread.

THIRST: Thirst indicates an emotional need. *See also* individual beverage listings.

THORN: A thorn is representative of annoyances and inconveniences that need to be settled before a project or plan can proceed. *See also* Rose.

THREAD: A thread suggests an idea that proves fruitful. If threads are hanging from garments, someone has some loose ends to tie up. *See also* Needle, Patch, Sewing, and Thimble.

THROAT: If sore, someone has difficulty expressing feelings.

THRONE: A throne is a symbol of authority. *See also* King, Prince, Princess, and Queen.

THUMB: If given a thumbs-up or a thumbs-down, it is a literal translation. If not, does someone feel pressed, like they're under someone else's thumb?

THUNDER: Thunder foretells rumors that will come to nothing. *See also* Cloud, Lightning, Rain, Sky, and Storm.

TIARA: You are royalty for a day! Pamper yourself. *See also* Princess and Queen.

TICKLE: A tickle means happiness and elation through a pleasant surprise.

TIDAL WAVE: A tidal wave suggests overwhelming emotions. *See also* Ocean and Tide.

TIDE: A tide implies life's ebb and flow, particularly the emotional aspects of life. *See also* Ocean and Tidal Wave.

TIGER: A tiger symbolizes power, strength, and energy.

TIGHTS: Someone is too narrow-minded in their thinking and needs to loosen up a bit. *See also* Pantyhose.

TIP: A tip is a symbol of giving and receiving. To receive a tip is a sign that someone may benefit from heeding good advice. To give a tip implies someone is in a position to make a positive difference in another's life. *See also* Waitstaff.

TOILET: Dreaming of a toilet indicates the ridding of unwanted emotional stress. *See also* Bathroom.

TOMATO: A tomato is a lucky symbol denoting happiness and love. *See also* Food.

TONGUE: Beware of idle gossip. *See also* Dentist and Mouth.

TOOTH: To lose a tooth in a dream suggests maturity through life experiences. *See also* Dentist and Mouth.

TOPAZ: Topaz is a warning sign to proceed cautiously in business affairs. *See also* Gems.

TORCH: Is someone carrying a torch for someone else? It

can also be an indication of leadership abilities if a torch is passed to you. *See also* Fire.

TORNADO: Expect a sudden and dramatic change in domestic matters. *See also* Storm.

TORPEDO: Someone is focused on goals and may enjoy favorable results. Their efforts may make an impact. *See also* Explosion, Ship, and Submarine.

TOWEL: Throwing in a towel signifies resignation. If drying hands with a towel, it implies a job was done well. *See also* Bath, Bathroom, and Tub.

TOWER: Ambitious goals are not easily attainable, but they are not totally out of reach.

TOY: Indulge in a hobby for a while. All work and no play is no fun at all.

TRAFFIC: Traffic represents how someone is navigating

through life. Is someone in the fast lane or stuck in traffic? *See also* Car.

TRAILER (MOBILE HOME): It is time to end a relationship that is going nowhere. *See also* House.

TRAIN: Someone needs to stay on track and not let petty annoyances be a distraction. *See also* Railroad.

TRAPEZE: A trapeze is a symbol of a quick mind. Someone makes good decisions with little hesitation. *See also* Acrobat and Circus.

TREASURE: If treasure is found, someone will receive an award. If hunting for treasure, someone is looking for recognition. *See also* Gems, Gold, and Pirate.

TREES: Trees are a good omen of strength, endurance, prosperity, and growth. *See*

also Leaf and individual tree listings.

TRENCH: Someone is hiding something. If there is water in the trench, someone is concealing something for reasons of vanity and pride. *See also* Battle, Ditch, and Water.

TRIANGLE: A triangle is a symbol of the power and harmony of body, mind, and spirit.

TRIPLETS: Triplets indicate unexpected surprises. *See also* Baby.

TROPHY: To receive a trophy predicts triumphant achievement of a long-standing goal. *See also* Medal.

TRUCK: A truck represents feelings of carrying a heavy burden. If the truck is in motion, the feelings may pass quickly. If the truck is parked, it may take a little while

Gorilla Tactics

Actress and author Shirley MacLaine provides a marvelous example of how our dream selves can remind us that we are the creators of our own dreams. In her book, *It's All in the Playing*, she describes a recurring childhood dream in which she is being chased by a gorilla to the edge of an abyss. Choosing to confront the gorilla instead of jumping into the abyss, she asks him, "What do I do now?" Throwing up his hands, the gorilla replies, "I don't know, kid, it's your dream!"

before the feelings pass. *See also* Car.

TRUMPET: Toot your horn! Promote talents, because there is a receptive audience. *See also* Music.

TUB: A tub is a symbol of cleansing and the easing of sorrows. *See also* Bath, Bathroom, Bubbles, and Towel.

TUGBOAT: Extra responsibilities will slow someone's pace. *See also* Water.

TUNNEL: Someone is going through a tense time, but it is almost over.

TURKEY: A turkey implies someone who speaks loud and long but says little of value. *See also* Birds and Food.

TURNIP: A lost item may soon be found in an unusual place. *See also* Food.

TURQUOISE: Turquoise is a symbol of spiritual and emotional healing. *See also* Gems.

TURTLE: Have patience. Slow and steady wins the race.

TWINS: There are two sides of the story. *See also* Baby.

UMBRELLA: An umbrella represents shelter in a storm.

There will be arguments around you, but you will not be involved. *See also* Rain.

UMPIRE: Someone outside a situation will help settle a dispute. *See also* individual sport listings.

UNDERWATER: If struggling underwater, someone is under a lot of pressure. If moving underwater with ease, someone may be able to adapt to a new situation easily. *See also* Drowning and Swim.

UNDERWEAR: Personal, private issues need to be dealt with.

UNICORN: A unicorn is a symbol of purity and rarity.

UNICYCLE: Someone will journey alone as they move through changing circumstances. *See also* Bicycle.

UNIFORM: Wearing a uniform implies a period in which choices will not seem to be your own. To see someone else in uniform suggests you need more discipline in some area of your life. *See also* Officer.

UNIVERSE: The universe suggests all of creation and spiritual yearnings. *See also* Planets and Star.

UNIVERSITY: A university marks a place of higher learning, representing spiritual lessons and knowledge. *See also* School and Teacher.

UPHOLSTERY: If reupholstering furniture, make the best of what you've got until something better comes along.

U-TURN: If you make a U-turn, you may change your mind about something. If someone else makes the U-turn, an appointment may be canceled. *See also* Car and Passenger.

VACATION: Vacation has a literal meaning: travel for pleasure in the near future. *See also* Beach.

VACCINATION: Someone will be strengthened during a trying time. *See also* Medicine and Needle.

VACUUM CLEANER: Using a vacuum cleaner implies taking care of small domestic details. *See also* Housekeeper.

VALENTINE: Expect a gift from someone special.

VALLEY: Someone may be feeling overwhelmed by others. It is their own perspective, their own insecurity.

VARNISH: Has something been glossed over and made to look better than it actually is? Examine the fine print. *See also* Housekeeper.

VASE: An empty vase is a sign of hope and potential. A vase of flowers suggests a secret admirer. *See also* Flowers and individual flower listings.

VAULT: Personal matters are best kept private.

VEIL: If you see someone wearing a veil over their face, it warns of secrets being kept. If you are wearing the veil, don't give away too much information.

VELVET: Velvet represents indulgence in pleasures.

VEST: A vest suggests shyness.

VETERAN: A veteran is a symbol of one who has survived struggle. *See also* Battle.

VIOLET: The color violet represents knowledge, enlightenment, wisdom, and spiritual matters.

VIOLIN: A violin is a symbol of sympathy and compassion. *See also* Fiddle and Music.

VOLCANO: A volcano predicts strong emotions that will be unleashed. *See also* Lava.

VOLUNTEER: To volunteer one's services is a good omen that recent good deeds may be recognized and rewarded.

VULTURE: Someone hopes to gain through another's loss. *See also* Birds.

WAFFLE: To dream about a waffle suggests confusion and indecision. *See also* Food.

WAITSTAFF: Is someone waiting for something? It may be necessary to take action. *See also* Food, Restaurant, and Tip.

WALL: A wall marks an obstacle to be overcome.

WALLET: A wallet represents personal beliefs and a sense of identity.

WALNUT: Cracking open a walnut indicates a perplexing puzzle may soon be solved. Whole walnuts imply minor barriers to a solution. *See also* Food and Nut.

WALRUS: You may have difficulty expressing yourself and tend to blurt things out without thinking.

WAND: To use a magic wand portends great luck in your endeavors. *See also* Magic and Magician.

WAREHOUSE: Someone has many resources at their disposal, some of which they are presently unaware.

WATER: Water is indicative of cleansing and washing away of troubles.

WATERFALL: A waterfall means an abundance of good fortune. *See also* Water.

WATERMELON: Eating watermelon is a sign of happy, carefree days ahead. *See also* Food.

WAX: If someone is waxing something, they are honing talents. If someone dreams of candle wax, they may be depleting their energy, as in "burning a candle at both ends." *See also* Candle and Chandelier.

WEALTH: Wealth suggests acquired wisdom though years of experience. *See also* Bank, Jackpot, and Money.

WEATHER VANE: A weather vane indicates direction and guidance from a higher authority. *See also* Wind.

WEEDS: Get rid of unwanted elements before they begin to interfere with goals. *See also* Dandelion and Garden.

WELL: Resources of knowledge and information are accessible. *See also* Water.

WHALE: A big project that seems overwhelming at first will proceed smoothly once underway.

WHEEL: This is the wheel of life, the cycles and patterns.

WHEELBARROW: Through physical labor someone gains strength and confidence.

WHISKERS: If on a man, whiskers are a sign of wisdom. If on an animal, whiskers represent instincts. *See also* individual animal listings.

WHISTLE: To hear a whistle in a dream is a warning of an unexpected event.

WHITE: The color white represents purity of heart and clarity of mind.

WIDOW: A widow points out feelings of loneliness and loss for a short period of time followed by a new sense of strength. *See also* Death.

WIG: If wearing a wig, you are concerned with the thoughts and opinions of others. *See also* Hair.

WILLOW TREE: A willow tree suggests one who is flexible in their attitudes and not rigid in their beliefs. *See also* Leaf and Trees.

WIND: Situations are not settled at present. Things are subject to change without notice. *See also* Weather Vane and Windmill.

WINDMILL: A windmill in motion is a sign of growth and progress. An unmoving windmill is a sign of hesitation. *See also* Wind.

WINDOW: A window marks sight into the future. What was seen out of the window? *See also* Curtain.

WING: A wing is a symbol of protection and security. *See also* Airplane and Birds.

WINE: Wine signifies good times with new friends. If toasting with wine, it means a celebration of the rewards of hard work. *See also* Thirst.

WINK: Flirtation and fleeting romance are to be expected.

WISE MAN/WISE WOMAN: The archetype is represented by the part of personality that holds knowledge and wisdom of which you are unaware, sometimes manifesting as inspiration, intuition, or hunches.

WISHBONE: A wishbone is an omen of good luck. The dearest wish is at hand. *See also* Chickens, Duck, Food, Goose, and Turkey.

WOLF: If alone, the wolf represents self-reliance. If in a pack, it represents a sense of community and cooperation.

WOODS: Can't see the forest for the trees? Woods symbolize confusion and feeling lost. *See also* Leaf, Moss, Oak, and Trees.

WOUND: An open wound is a sign of unfinished business. A healing wound is a sign that difficult times are over. *See also* Medicine.

WRESTLE: Someone is struggling with a decision. Weigh the pros and cons carefully.

WRIST: A wrist indicates strength and flexibility in the face of adverse conditions.

WRITING: Writing indicates communication and self-expression. *See also* Diary, Ink, Letter, Page, Paper, Poem, Quill, and Signature.

X RAY: Someone has the ability to see through a deception. *See also* Medicine and Radiation.

XYLOPHONE: There is a wide range of possibilities from which to choose. What is most appealing? *See also* Music.

YACHT: A yacht signifies a period of abundance, but it may not last. Be thrifty! *See also* Ship and Water.

YAM: Eating yams predicts a change of routine. *See also* Food.

YARD: A front yard represents the person you are in public. A backyard represents your more personal, private side.

YAWN: Someone is bored with a situation. It's time to move on. *See also* Mouth.

YEAST: If left unchecked, a situation may get out of control. *See also* Bread and Food.

YELLOW: The color yellow represents clear thinking, logic, and the intellect.

YODEL: To hear yodeling in a dream predicts an unexpected communication from far away. *See also* Music and Sing.

Man or Butterfly?

The great Taoist master Chuang Tzu once dreamt that he was a butterfly fluttering here and there. In the dream, he had no awareness of his individuality as a person; he was only a butterfly. Suddenly, he awoke and found himself laying there, a person once again. But then he thought to himself, "Was I before a man who dreamt about being a butterfly, or am I now a butterfly who dreams about being a man?"

YOGA: Patience and flexibility in the face of a tense situation will win the day. *See also* Lotus.

YOLK: Inside an aloof person lies a heart of gold. Help draw this person out of their shell. *See also* Eggs.

YO-YO: Someone will go back on a promise.

ZEBRA: Remember that not everything is either black or white. Make room for compromise.

ZIPPER: Keep your mouth zipped! Hold your tongue when in the presence of gossips.

ZIRCON: Something seems too good to be true and that is exactly what it is. Don't be fooled by flashy appearances. *See also* Gems.

ZOO: A zoo signifies confusion. Too many unrelated elements are thrown together. *See also* individual animal listings.